HISTORY EARNED!

Houston Astros

World Champions

Katherine Grigsby, Layout & Design

ISBN: 978-1-940056-57-9 (HC)

Printed in the United States of America
www.kcisports.com

CONTENTS

WORLD SERIES CH

Houston Astros 2017 World Champions
AP Photo

UNFORGETTABLE

Houston Astros - World Champions!

Sounds pretty good doesn't it? Houston fans have waited an awfully long time to utter those words, and finally, the Astros are on top.

Let the celebration begin!

It is an honor to write an introduction to such a historic season. It's not easy to win in the big leagues, but when you are able to get 101 W's in the regular season you know you are doing something right.

The Astros have been close before, but for whatever reason weren't able to get over the hump. Until now. When General Manager Jeff Luhnow announced the trade for Justin Verlander, Houston fans knew the Astros were going all in on the 2017 season. The excitement of the Verlander trade and the success of the Astros was a pleasant distraction for thousands of Texas residents trying to piece their lives back together after Hurricane Harvey. With devastation and destruction all around them Houston fans never stopped supporting their team.

In the following pages we proudly bring you on a trip down memory lane of this championship season that came to its jubilant conclusion in Game 7 in Los Angeles. History Earned provides Astros fans the best view in the house of all the ups and downs of the season and gives you an inside look at the incredible World Series win against a very talented Los Angeles Dodgers team.

Our heartfelt congratulations go out to owner Jim Crane, General Manager Jeff Luhnow, Manager A.J. Hinch and his staff, and the entire team on their accomplishments this season. Celebrate this season Houston fans, and save this book to revisit the Astros' magical moments and unforgettable team – both stars and role players – who rewarded your faith with the franchises first ever World Championship.

Congratulations Astros! Let's do it again soon.

Sincerely,

KCI Sports Publishing

Astros Enter Spring Training Cautiously Optimistic

Astros outfielder Norichika Aoki (right) stretches with pitcher Dallas Keuchel during a spring training workout.
AP Photo

This is the season Astros general manager Jeff Luhnow envisioned almost from the moment he was hired six offseasons ago.

Houston has reached the point in their rebuilding process where it simply isn't good enough anymore to post winning records like they did last year. A slow start to the season (as opposed to the hot start that carried them to the playoffs in 2015) doomed them, but this year's roster, with another year of experience and even more veteran leadership in the clubhouse should

Astros infielder Marwin Gonzalez prepares for a batting practice session during spring training. *AP Photo*

not have a problem getting back to the postseason.

The Astros enter Spring Training cautiously optimistic that two of their top three starters -- Dallas Keuchel and Lance McCullers -- are healthy. Both finished last season on the disabled list with shoulder and arm issues. Had they been healthy, Houston probably would have gone to the playoffs.

"We're healthy," Luhnow said, "but we know there's a long way to go."

That's probably also true of 2017, even though the remainder of the roster has been significantly reshaped.

No general manager had a better offseason than Luhnow, who added catcher Brian McCann, starting pitcher Charlie Morton and outfielders Carlos Beltran, Josh Reddick and Norichika Aoki in a flurry of moves.

Combine those with the additions of third baseman Alex Bregman and first baseman Yulieski Gurriel last year after the All-Star break, and Houston barely resemble the 2016 team that started 7-17 and needed 73 games to get above .500 for good.

"If we can avoid getting off to a bad start like we did last year, I think chances

are good that we're going to be seeing baseball in October here," Luhnow said.

He offered a hat tip of Astros owner Jim Crane, who has approved the highest payroll in team history -- around $120 million.

"I gotta give our ownership group a round of applause for allowing us the resources to go after that many players," Luhnow said. "We feel like this sets us up very well for the next four to five years. Not only that, we maintain the medium and long-term health of this organization."

When Crane hired Luhnow in December 2011, the owner promised to give his GM the resources and freedom to do a dramatic teardown and rebuild. Houston averaged 103 losses in the three seasons before a surprise playoff appearance -- the franchise's first in a decade -- in '15.

"If we think about it as an organization, how fortunate are we to have three years in a row [with] rookies coming up like George Springer, Carlos Correa and Alex Bregman," Luhnow said. "Those are three elite-level players that are going to be here for awhile."

Looking back on it, the Astros surprised even themselves by making the playoffs in 2015. Despite everything, they were in contention until the final week last season. One problem: Houston was 4-15 against the Texas Rangers, 37-20 against the rest of the AL West.

"We understand that the AL West goes through the Rangers," Luhnow said. "We haven't been good enough against them."

All of which seems to set the stage for 2017.

Astros third baseman Yuli Gurriel stretches out his arm during a spring training workout. *AP Photo*

APRIL 3, 2017   MINUITE MAID PARK   HOUSTON, TEXAS
HOUSTON ASTROS 3 • SEATTLE MARINERS 0

Keuchel leads Houston to Opening Day win

Above: Astros starting pitcher Dallas Keuchel delivers the first pitch of the season. *AP Photo*

Left: Center fielder George Springer hits a leadoff solo home run. *AP Photo*

HOUSTON -- After a terrible 2016, Dallas Keuchel desperately wanted to get off to a good start.

He did just that, allowing two hits over seven innings before Luke Gregerson and Ken Giles completed the three-hitter for the Houston Astros in an opening 3-0 win over the Seattle Mariners.

Keuchel (1-0) went 9-12 with a 4.55

The Astros Alex Bregman slides safely into second base as the ball gets away from Seattle second baseman Robinson Cano. *AP Photo*

ERA last year after winning the AL Cy Young Award in 2015. He struck out four in winning on opening day for the third year in a row.

Last year, he didn't pitch after Aug. 27 because of shoulder inflammation.

"I know what I'm capable of doing when I'm healthy. I know how bad I can be when I'm not healthy," he said. "I knew I was good coming in and I was just hoping to get the team off to a good start."

Manager A.J. Hinch thinks Keuchel's struggles last season gave his ace an extra edge entering this year.

"I think he comes into this season with a little chip on his shoulder, and rightfully so," Hinch said. "For him on opening day I think he wants to set a tone for the club. I think he wanted to show that every five days when he gets the ball our team is going to rally behind him. It's certainly nice to have that as opposed to me sitting up here explaining a rough outing. And he responded in incredible fashion."

Gregerson allowed a hit and Giles walked one with three strikeouts for the save.

George Springer became Houston's first player since Terry Puhl in 1980 to lead off the first game with a home run. Carlos Correa homered and drove in two runs as Houston won on opening day for the fifth straight year.

Felix Hernandez (0-1), making his 10th opening day start, allowed two runs and five hits while striking out six in five innings before leaving with tightness in a groin. Hernandez pulled up after racing to cover first base for the second out of the fourth inning on Josh Reddick's grounder. Hernandez was looked at by trainers and threw a couple of warmup pitches before finishing the inning.

Springer hit his 10th leadoff home run. Correa made it 2-0 in the fourth with a 449-foot drive that sailed over the train tracks atop left field, then hit a sacrifice in the sixth.

Keuchel retired his first 10 batters before Robinson Cano singled and Nelson Cruz walked. A two-out walk by Danny Valencia loaded the bases, but Keuchel retired Leonys Martin on a groundout.

Talk of the Town

Springer patrolling centerfield. *AP Photo*

George Springer sat alone behind the podium, with a sea of strangers staring at him, all wanting to ask questions.

He looked around the room, leaned back, closed his eyes, and remembered the days that he would be terrified to be in this situation.

He absolutely hated to talk.

When he was a kid, he would sit in the back of the class, hoping the teacher would never call him. When he went to the University of Connecticut, he enrolled in classes where there were no presentations. When he went out to eat, he'd simply point at the item on the menu.

"I was the guy who didn't talk," says Springer, who hit the biggest home run in the Houston Astros' history in Game 2, a two-run shot in the 11th inning that provided the club's first-ever World Series victory - a 7-6 triumph that evened the Series 1-1 with the Dodgers.

"I would sit in the back. I would avoid speaking at all costs up until I was 18 or 19 in college. I didn't even like to order food on the phone. I was just so scared to do it."

Springer, you see, has a stuttering problem. He had it his whole life. He doesn't ever remember taking speech therapy, or getting outside assistance.

He just avoided talking.

"When I was around my friends, it didn't seem to bother them. I would just talk, and if I did [stutter] they would wait until I was done, and then just continued the conversation."

It wasn't until three years ago, when Springer was emerging as a star, and the cover subject of the famous 2014 Sports Illustrated that predicted the Astros would be World Series champs in 2017, that Springer realized he could no longer hide.

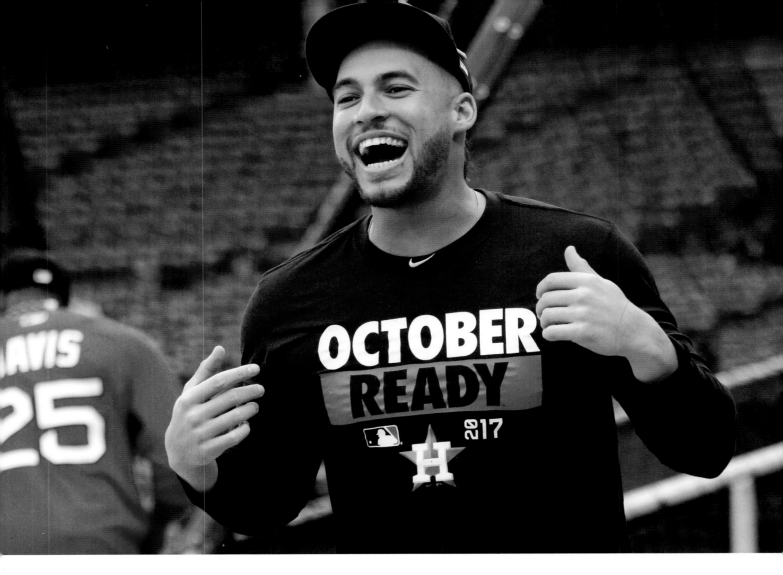

George Springer laughs with teammates during a workout prior to the World Series. *AP Photo*

"I was talking to a group of kids in New York," said Springer, a spokesman for SAY, the Stuttering Association for the Young, "and I kind of had an epiphany that I'm involved in this organization for one reason. And that's to help anybody I can.

"I want kids or adults to see I'm a normal person. I just happen to stutter. Seeing these kids and the pain they go through because they feel bullied, and they feel isolated, is sad.

"I decided right then and there, "You know what, I'm going to expose myself.""

So Springer began talking. He became one of the faces of the franchise. He was mic'd up at the All-Star Game while in the field. And there he was at the World Series, talking to a room full of reporters, sometimes stumbling over a word, but sitting confidently, atop the world.

"I've become more comfortable talking," says Springer, who hit a career-high 34 homers, all out of the leadoff spot. "I was like, I can't tell somebody to do something if I'm not going to go out and do it myself."

Now, if everything goes according to plan, he'll be on a parade float in downtown Houston in a week, grabbing every microphone he can find.

"I can't wait to tell the world," Springer says, "that the Houston Astros are World Series champs.

"That's my dream."

MAY 3, 2017   MINUITE MAID PARK   HOUSTON, TEXAS
HOUSTON ASTROS 10 • TEXAS RANGERS 1

Gonzalez, Astros rough up Rangers

Above: Marwin Gonzalez slides into third base safely ahead of the tag by Rangers third baseman Joey Gallo during the second inning. *AP Photo*

Left: Shortstop Carlos Correa turns a double-play while avoiding the slide of the Rangers Jonathan Lucroy. *AP Photo*

HOUSTON -- Marwin Gonzalez hit yet another big homer against the Texas Rangers, and the Houston Astros are looking like the kings of the Lone Star State this season.

Gonzalez homered for the fourth time in his last three games, Carlos Correa had four hits and the Astros beat the Rangers 10-1 on.

Gonzalez had two hits and smashed

Astros third baseman Alex Bregman congratulates teammate Brian McCann after a McCann home run in the second inning. *AP Photo*

a two-run homer off the batter's eye in center in the sixth inning for a 6-1 lead. He hit two home runs against Texas on Tuesday, including a go-ahead grand slam in the eighth that rallied Houston to an 8-7 win. He also homered against Oakland on Sunday.

Correa and Brian McCann sparked a four-run second inning with solo homers off starter Nick Martinez (0-1). Correa finished 4 for 5 and a triple shy of the cycle.

"I didn't think he was going to go a whole season without having a breakout night like this," Astros manager A.J. Hinch said of Correa, who raised his average to .255.

"What happens in baseball is we put too much emphasis on the cumulative stats, and you forget some of the quality plate appearances that come along the way. A night like tonight, we expect him to have every night, but it's the big leagues, and you can't do that."

With their fourth straight win, the Astros have the best record in baseball at 19-9, fueled by a 15-4 mark against the AL West. They matched their best

28-game start in franchise history, set by the 2006 club.

The Rangers, meanwhile, are hanging around the bottom of the division with an 11-17 record. They matched a season high with three errors and have lost five straight and eight of their last nine games on the road.

"We need some momentum," catcher Jonathan Lucroy said. "We need a stopper on the mound who can shut it down for us so the lineup can score some runs. We've got to play better all around, we've got to hit better, we've got to pitch better, we've got to play defense better. Right now, we're not doing that."

Charlie Morton (3-2) allowed a run and five hits in six innings, striking out eight and walking two. The Rangers were hitless until Rougned Odor doubled in the fourth inning.

Josh Reddick added a two-run homer off Anthony Bass in the eighth.

Every Astros hitter reached base except for Jose Altuve, who had a rare 0-for-5 night. Gonzalez, Correa, George Springer and Alex Bregman all had multihit games. Houston improved to 15-1 when scoring four runs or more.

"Three wins against Texas -- it's good to win the series," said the Astros George Springer. "Obviously, they've beaten us pretty good over the last few years, but that's in the past. It's a good series win for us."

Astros starting pitcher Charlie Morton threw six strong innings to pick up his third win of the year. *AP Photo*

Royals first baseman Eric Hosmer
slides in under the tag of Jose Altuve.
AP Photo

JUNE 5, 2017   KAUFFMAN STADIUM   KANSAS CITY, MISSOURI
HOUSTON ASTROS 7 • KANSAS CITY ROYALS 3

Astros Win 11ᵗʰ Straight

Norichika Aoki delivers an RBI single during the second inning. *AP Photo*

KANSAS CITY, Mo. -- The Houston Astros scored early and late to keep up their winning ways.

Yuli Gurriel hit a three-run homer, Brian McCann had a two-run shot and the Astros beat the Kansas City Royals 7-3 for their 11th straight win.

It's the longest winning streak in the majors this season and one shy of the Astros' record. They won 12 straight in 1999 and 2004.

McCann homered in the fourth after Marwin Gonzalez walked to lead off the inning. He had been 1 for 16 in five games since returning from a concussion.

"I haven't been swinging the bat well since I've come back off the DL," McCann said. "I've made some minor adjustments

and was able to drive the ball to left-center and when I'm doing that, it's a good sign."

Gurriel homered in the ninth off Kelvin Herrera. He has gone deep in back-to-back games and has 10 RBI during a six-game hitting streak.

"We got after them early and then they put on a little bit of a push and it got really close," Astros manager A.J. Hinch said. "Then obviously Yuli's home run off of Herrera was a big punch for us."

McCann started a two-run second inning with a one-out double and scored on Nori Aoki's single. George Springer's two-out single scored Gurriel, who had walked.

Houston has won 11 consecutive road games, which is a franchise record. The team is 22-6 away from home this season.

"We don't sit there feeling like, `Boy they look like they are going to win tonight," Royals manager Ned Yost said. "But you look at their team and what they're doing, I'm sure that's their attitude and their feeling."

Astros starter Mike Fiers (3-2) worked five innings plus two batters. He was charged with two runs, seven hits and a walk. Fiers is 6-0 in his past 10 road starts dating to Aug. 20.

"You can throw strikes, but they've got to be in good spots, especially against a team that swings a lot like these guys," Fiers said. "They come out swinging early, so pitch one is huge."

The Royals scored a pair of runs in the second. Brandon Moss doubled to score Eric Hosmer,

Astros designated hitter Carlos Beltran works on his bubble blowing skills between innings. *AP Photo*

Yuli Gurriel celebrates with Brian McCann after hitting a three-run home run during the ninth inning. *AP Photo*

while Alcides Escobar's bunt single got Mike Moustakas home.

Rookie Jorge Bonifacio homered off James Hoyt in the seventh to trim the lead to 4-3.

The Royals had Hosmer at third and Moustakas at first with none out in the sixth, but failed to score. Moss and Escobar struck out to end the inning.

Ian Kennedy (0-6) took the loss, giving up four runs, six hits and three walks over five innings.

Marwin Gonzalez, right, high-fives Carlos Correa after Correa hit a solo home run as Evan Gattis prepares to step to the plate. *AP Photo*

JULY 9, 2017   ROGERS CENTRE   TORANTO, ONTARIO
HOUSTON ASTROS 19 • TORANTO BLUE JAYS 1

Astros blast Jays for 60th win

Carlos Correa watches the flight of his second-inning home run off Blue Jays starting pitcher J.A. Happ. *AP Photo*

TORONTO -- Carlos Correa, Jose Altuve and the Houston Astros put on quite an All-Star performance.

Correa homered twice and drove in a career-high five runs, Altuve got three more hits, and the Astros romped into the break, battering the Toronto Blue Jays 19-1.

The runaway leaders in the American League West became just the fifth team in the past 40 years to reach 60 wins before the All-Star Game, according to

Houston second baseman Jose Altuve hits one of three Astro home runs during a five run second inning. *AP Photo*

the Elias Sports Bureau. They joined the 1998 Yankees, 2001 Mariners, 2003 Braves and this year's Los Angeles Dodgers, who got there Saturday.

At 60-29, Houston heads into the break with a 16½-game lead over the Texas Rangers and Los Angeles Angels.

"I feel like we have a really good team," Correa said. "From 1 through 9,

"It's nice to say we should keep this going, but we need as many people to rest up here in the next four days," he said.

A day after his career-high 15-game hitting streak ended, Correa had four hits. The All-Star shortstop hit the 20-home run mark with his second of the day for his fifth career multihomer game and second this season.

Altuve, a fellow All-Star, Yuli Gurriel and Evan Gattis also homered for Houston. Altuve had three hits for the fifth consecutive game -- becoming the ninth major leaguer to do so in more than a century and the first since George Brett's record-tying six-game streak for Kansas City in 1976.

Gattis drove in four runs with two hits as Houston scored at least 19 runs for the fourth time in club history.

Brad Peacock (7-1) pitched six innings of shutout ball, holding the Blue Jays to five hits while walking five. After appearing on a 2013 Houston team that won just 51 games all season, the right-hander said the current feeling around the clubhouse makes the struggles worth it.

"Being on those teams makes it a lot more special ... and it's all paying off now," he said.

Ezequiel Carrera homered with two outs in the Toronto ninth to establish a new career high with seven. The drive denied Houston the chance to top the largest shutout win in team history, 15-0 at Montreal on April 26, 1998.

J.A. Happ (3-6) lasted four innings, matching his shortest outing of the season and picking up his second loss to Houston in eight starts against his former team. The left-hander gave up seven hits and six runs.

"I wasn't very crisp today, and against that lineup, especially, you need to be," he said.

we can do damage, so today we showed what we're capable of."

The Astros posted the most lopsided win in team history. Even in the midst of a 14-5 run the past three weeks, manager A.J. Hinch said he felt the break comes at a good time for his club.

Starting pitcher Mike Fiers went seven innings to pick up his first win since July 21.
AP Photo

AUGUST 23, 2017   MINUITE MAID PARK   HOUSTON, TEXAS

HOUSTON ASTROS 6 • WASHINGTON NATIONALS 1

Astros power past Nationals

Astros center fielder Jake Marisnick launches his fifteenth home run of the season during the fifth inning. *AP Photo*

HOUSTON -- The Houston Astros used a big eighth inning to put a close game out of reach and get their first win against the Washington Nationals since 2012 in a matchup of division leaders.

Alex Bregman hit a three-run homer and Jake Marisnick and Max Stassi added solo shots to help the American League West-leading Astros to a 6-1 win.

The victory snaps a nine-game losing streak to the Nationals, who lead the National League East, and is just Houston's

Astros first baseman Yuli Gurriel is unable to make the catch as Nationals left fielder Howie Kendrick dives back safely to first base during the third inning. *AP Photo*

Hinch said. "It was nice to break out and get a couple of runs."

Houston starter Mike Fiers (8-8) yielded four hits and one run in seven strong innings to get his first win since July 21. Fiers was in command from the start, looking much better than he had in his last four starts when he allowed a combined 24 hits and 20 runs.

"He had a great game," Hinch said. "He was really good from the very beginning with his fastball. I think it was the best fastball I've seen out of him in a while. I know he felt really good and he was executing his pitches in and out."

The game was tied at 1 with one out in the fifth when Marisnick sent a curveball from Edwin Jackson (4-3) into left-center field for his 15th homer.

In the eighth, Stassi launched a towering shot to the train tracks atop left field to push the lead to 3-1. Marisnick singled and George Springer walked before Bregman's home run made it 6-1.

Bregman loved that the Astros did all of the damage in the eighth inning with two outs.

"It was huge," he said. "Early in the year we did a lot of that. We did a lot of two-out hitting and that's one of the things that I think this team is really good at. And we've got to keep that up if we want to win ball games."

Jackson allowed six hits and two runs in six innings for the loss.

Andrew Stevenson got things going for Washington when he doubled with one out in the third inning before a single by Howie Kendrick. The Nationals took a 1-0 lead when Stevenson scored on a sacrifice fly by Wilmer Difo.

Jose Altuve got a triple to start Houston's fourth when Stevenson ran in front of Michael Taylor in center field and just missed making the catch on his fly ball. Houston tied it when Altuve scored on a sacrifice fly by Josh Reddick.

"Jackson, he threw a heck of a game," manager Dusty Baker said. "He left 2-1 and really it should have been one run from the home run by Marisnick. He threw the ball well."

second win in the last 15 games against Washington.

"We've got guys that have been putting up pretty good at-bats," manager A.J.

"We hand him the ball and the entire room knows we have a chance to win."

–Houston manager A.J. Hinch

Dallas Keuchel won the 2015 Cy Young award. *AP Photo*

Dallas Keuchel is tired of talking about his success against the New York Yankees.

Unlike the pitcher, manager A.J. Hinch didn't shy away from singing Keuchel's praises for his work against the Yankees. He joked that the lefty will probably feel better when he takes the mound and sees players in Yankees uniforms. But he was quick to point out that Keuchel's success certainly hasn't been limited to games against New York.

"I know there's a confidence level," Hinch said. "And to be honest with you, when Dallas is right, he's confident against anybody. I don't think who the names are or who the jersey is, he knows he can get anybody out in the league."

But Keuchel has pitched better than most against the Yankees in recent years, going 4-2 with a 1.41 ERA and 45 strikeouts in six regular-season starts. His biggest win to date against them came in the 2015 AL wild-card game when he and the then-upstart Astros got a 3-0 win in the Bronx. "For that win in the wild-card game, it wasn't just special for me and the validation, it was special for everybody to go into New York and play that well," he said. "But now we look back on it and it's probably one of the most magical times that I'll have in my career and it's something I'll never forget, for sure."

Keuchel gets the nod in the opener after pitching behind Justin Verlander in the ALDS. Verlander, who was acquired

Keuchel takes time out from his warm-up to play with a security dog before a game against the Washington Nationals. *AP Photo*

on Aug. 31, made his first career relief appearance to help eliminate the Red Sox in Game 4.

Hinch sees Keuchel and Verlander as 1A and 1B in his rotation, so who pitched first wasn't that big of a deal to him.

"Dallas is really good, so I'm not the least bit hesitant on starting him," Hinch said. "When we made the move to pitch Verlander in Game 4 out of relief we had the backdrop that Dallas was going to start Game 5. So I have all the confidence in the world."

Keuchel won the AL Cy Young Award in 2015 when he went 20-8 with a 2.48 ERA before struggling last season, with a 9-12 record and 4.55 ERA. He bounced back this year despite neck issues, posting a 14-5 record with a 2.90 ERA to help the Astros run away with the AL West title.

He built off that in his first start this postseason when he yielded three hits and a run in 5 2/3 innings to help Houston to an 8-2 win over the Red Sox in Game 2 of the ALDS. That made him 3-0 with a 2.29 ERA in four postseason appearances with three starts.

"Dallas Keuchel has been remarkable as an Astro, he's been remarkable in my three years here," Hinch said. "We hand him the ball and the entire room knows we have a chance to win."

Cameron Maybin, left,
celebrates with Carlos Correa,
right, after the team's 5-3 win
over the Seattle Mariners.
AP Photo

SEPTEMBER 5, 2017   SAFECO FIELD   SEATTLE, WASHINGTON
HOUSTON ASTROS 3 • SEATTLE MARINERS 1

New guys Verlander, Maybin lift Astros over Mariners 3-1

Justin Verlander had seven strikeouts in his first start for the Astros. *AP Photo*

SEATTLE -- The only comparison Justin Verlander could come up with for his Houston Astros debut was opening day.

The nerves. The excitement. The desire to be at his best.

"The unknown. New team. Don't really want to let everyone down," Verlander said. "But these guys have made the process pretty easy on me so far fitting in and making me feel right at home as quickly as possible."

Cameron Maybin delivers a clutch two-run home run during the seventh inning. It was the first hit of the game for Houston. *AP Photo*

Verlander could find a home anywhere with the kind of performance he delivered Tuesday night, throwing six strong innings to beat the Seattle Mariners 3-1 after Cameron Maybin hit a two-run homer in the seventh for Houston's first hit.

It was the first time in 381 career regular-season starts that Verlander, a six-time All-Star, pitched for someone other than the Detroit Tigers. Even if his uniform colors were slightly different, his fastball and ability to dominate a

a purpose," Houston manager A.J. Hinch said. "I don't think he had great feel for his breaking ball early in the count. Had a really good fastball and he went to it."

With fiance Kate Upton in the stands, Verlander (11-8) allowed six hits and struck out seven while completing six innings for the 10th straight start.

His only costly mistake was a 3-2 pitch that Kyle Seager hit for a home run leading off the fourth. Seattle threatened in the sixth when Robinson Cano opened the inning by hitting a liner off Verlander's right wrist. Nelson Cruz followed with a single, but Seager grounded into a double play and Mitch Haniger struck out with Cano on third to end the threat.

The final pitch from the 2011 AL MVP was a 99 mph fastball that fanned Haniger.

"That was as impressive a finish of an outing as we could ask for, especially in the big moments where the inning starts out with runners on base," Hinch said. "He never gets out of control."

Joe Musgrove threw two innings of scoreless relief and Ken Giles pitched the ninth for his 29th save.

With all the attention on Verlander's first game for a team other than the Tigers, it was another deadline acquisition that sent Houston to its sixth straight victory. Maybin's drive with one out in the seventh snapped a 1-all tie.

Maybin arrived on Aug. 31 after being claimed off waivers from the Los Angeles Angels.

"This team has been playing great team baseball and everybody has something to do with the success. I'm just trying to fit in to the mold of trying to help out," Maybin said.

Seattle starter Ariel Miranda threw 112 pitches over six hitless innings that included six walks -- three of which led to Houston's first run in the third on Alex Bregman's sacrifice fly.

James Pazos (4-5) relieved in the seventh and walked Brian McCann with one out. Pazos was replaced by Emilio Pagan, who left a 3-2 pitch in the middle of the plate and Maybin hit his eighth homer of the season.

game were the same.

It wasn't Verlander at his best. But it was a very good beginning in the latest chapter of his career, with the top team in the American League.

"We need to get to know him quickly. And to see his mannerisms, to see how he competes, he throws every pitch with

Houston Strong

The Houston Strong patch worn by Astro players. *AP Photo*

On August 25th, 2017 hundreds of thousands of lives along the Texas coast were changed forever. That was the day Hurricane Harvey made landfall. The category 4 storm brought torrential rains and 130-mph winds that hammered those in its path without mercy.

The Astros' postseason run has been a welcome diversion for residents of Houston, where Harvey's floodwaters damaged about 100,000 homes. Thousands of Texans have been unable to return to their ruined houses and are still living with relatives or in motels. Some streets and vacant lots still contain piles of debris from mucked-out buildings.

The storm affected the Astros, too. Although their ballpark, Minute Maid Park, survived Harvey largely unscathed, the team was forced to play three "home"

games in St. Petersburg, Florida, in late August as floodwaters crippled parts of the city.

After they returned to Houston, many Astros players spent a rare day off at a downtown convention center, meeting with Harvey evacuees. And at every game since they have worn a "Houston Strong" patch on their uniforms -- a nod to the slogan the city adopted after the storm.

The team has no shortage of civic heroes, from pint-sized powerhouse Jose Altuve -- at 5 feet 6 inches, he's the majors' shortest player -- to ace pitcher Justin Verlander, who arrived via a trade from the Detroit Tigers a week after Hurricane Harvey hit. Earlier this month Verlander announced a fund, launched with $100,000 of his own money, to provide financial assistance to veterans and military families impacted by the hurricane.

Some fans will tell you that after seeing their lives upended by a hurricane that dumped a record 51 inches of rain on their city, they deserve a World Series title.

"Everywhere I go, the people who have been affected by this storm, they come up and say thank you. Folks really see themselves as a part of this club," said Reid Ryan, the Astros' president of business operations. "It really would be great if we could somehow catch magic in a bottle and win this thing for them.

"In a way we've become -- to use a wrestling term -- the people's champ," he added. "We're the team that I think folks around the country are rooting for because of what we've been through."

"If you understand what we went through with Harvey, to be able to give back to the fans -- it's incredible," said former Astro Craig Biggio, now a special assistant to the team's general manager, after his team's dramatic ALCS Game 7 victory over the New York Yankees.

"The people here needed this."

Jose Altuve comes back out of the dugout for a curtain call after his third home run of the game. *AP Photo*

AMERICAN LEAGUE DIVISION SERIES

OCTOBER 5, 2017   MINUTE MAID PARK   HOUSTON, TEXAS
HOUSTON ASTROS 8 • BOSTON RED SOX 2

Altuve leads Astros past Red Sox in ALDS opener

Designated hitter Evan Gattis shatters his bat as he hits a double during the fourth inning. *AP Photo*

HOUSTON -- The major league batting champion put on an unprecedented show of power.

Buoyed by chants of "MVP" in each trip to the plate, the 5-foot-6 Jose Altuve hit three home runs as Houston roughed up Chris Sale and the Boston Red Sox 8-2 in Game 1 of the AL Division Series.

Altuve hit solo homers in the first and fifth innings off Sale. He connected again in the seventh off reliever Austin Maddox to give Houston a quick boost in the best-of-five series.

It was just the 10th time a player hit three homers in a postseason game, and first since Pablo Sandoval for the Giants in the 2012 World Series opener against

Jose Altuve celebrates his fifth inning home run with teammate Carlos Correa. *AP Photo*

Detroit. Babe Ruth did it twice.

"I told him the last time I've seen three home runs in a game was Pablo Sandoval and I gave up two of them, so I'm glad there's somebody new that's done it," winning pitcher Justin Verlander said.

Altuve became the first Astros player to hit three homers in one game since 2007, when Carlos Lee did it in the regular season. He seemed as surprised as anyone else that he was now in a category with the Sultan of Swat, Reggie Jackson and Albert Pujols.

"I hit one and I was like: `Wow,'" he said. "And the second one is like: `Wow, what's going on here?'"

And his thoughts after the third?

"I got to wake up," he said, flashing a huge grin.

Verlander pitched six effective innings and improved to 6-0 since Houston got him in late trade with Detroit. He is 5-0 with a 2.24 ERA in nine career starts in the division series.

Sale, the major league strikeout leader, was tagged for seven runs in five-plus innings of his postseason debut.

"First off, how good is Jose Altuve?" Houston manager A.J. Hinch asked. "It's incredible to watch him step up and be every bit the star that we needed today. It's hard to describe in different ways."

Alex Bregman and Altuve hit back-to-back homers in the first inning, making Sale look a bit rattled. The Red Sox tied it up by scoring a run each in the second and fourth innings before Marwin Gonzalez lined a two-run double in the fourth for a 4-2 lead.

There were two outs in the fifth inning when Altuve connected again to push the lead to 5-2 and make him the third player in franchise history with a multihomer game in the postseason, joining Carlos Correa and Carlos Beltran.

The crowd of 43,402, which included Hall of Famers Nolan Ryan, Jeff Bagwell and Craig Biggio, waved bright orange towels as Altuve trotted around the bases.

BOX SCORE

	1	2	3	4	5	6	7	8	9		R	H	E
BOS	0	1	0	1	0	0	0	0	0		2	8	0
HOU	2	0	0	2	1	2	1	0	-		8	12	0

RED SOX

HITTERS	AB	R	H	RBI	BB	K	AVG
X. Bogaerts-SS	4	0	0	0	0	1	.000
E. Nunez-DH	1	0	0	0	0	0	.000
H. Ramirez-PH-DH	3	0	2	0	0	0	.667
A. Benintendi-LF	4	0	1	0	0	1	.250
M. Betts-RF	4	1	2	0	0	0	.500
M. Moreland-1B	3	1	1	0	1	0	.333
D. Pedroia-2B	3	0	0	0	1	0	.000
R. Devers-3B	3	0	1	0	0	2	.000
S. Leon-C	4	0	2	1	0	1	.000
J. Bradley Jr.-CF	3	0	0	0	0	1	.000
TEAM	**32**	**2**	**8**	**2**	**2**	**6**	

ASTROS

HITTERS	AB	R	H	RBI	BB	K	AVG
G. Springer-CF	4	0	0	0	0	3	.000
A. Bregman-3B	4	1	2	1	0	1	.500
J. Altuve-2B	4	3	3	3	0	0	.750
C. Correa-SS	4	0	0	0	0	0	.000
E. Gattis-DH	3	2	2	0	1	0	.667
D. Fisher-PR-DH	0	0	0	0	0	0	.000
J. Reddick-RF	3	2	2	0	1	1	.667
Y. Gurriel-1B	4	0	1	0	0	0	.250
M. Gonzalez-LF	4	0	1	2	0	2	.250
B. McCann-C	4	0	1	2	0	1	.250
TEAM	**34**	**8**	**12**	**8**	**2**	**8**	

RED SOXS

PITCHERS	IP	H	R	ER	BB	K	HR	ERA
C. Sale (L, 0-1)	5.0	9	7	7	1	6	3	12.60
J. Kelly	1.0	2	0	0	0	1	0	0.00
A. Maddox	1.0	1	1	1	1	1	1	9.00
R. Porcello	1.0	0	0	0	0	0	0	0.00
TEAM	**8.0**	**12**	**8**	**8**	**2**	**8**	**4**	

ASTROS

PITCHERS	IP	H	R	ER	BB	K	HR	ERA
Verlander (W, 1-0)	6.0	6	2	2	3	3	0	3.00
C. Devenski	1.0	0	0	0	0	2	0	0.00
W. Harris	0.2	2	0	0	0	0	0	0.00
F. Liriano	0.1	0	0	0	0	0	0	0.00
J. Musgrove	1.0	0	0	0	0	1	0	0.00
TEAM	**9.0**	**8**	**2**	**2**	**2**	**6**	**0**	

Sale never got into a rhythm and was chased after walking Josh Reddick with no outs in the sixth. The left-hander was tagged for nine hits and matched a season high for most runs allowed.

"Anytime he mislocated, particularly in the middle of the plate, they made him pay for it," manager John Farrell said.

Jose Altuve scores on teammate Carlos Correa's double during the sixth inning.   *AP Photo*

AMERICAN LEAGUE DIVISION SERIES

OCTOBER 6, 2017 · MINUTE MAID PARK · HOUSTON, TEXAS

HOUSTON ASTROS 8 • BOSTON RED SOX 2

Astros rout Red Sox, take 2-0 series lead

Astros shortstop Carlos Correa drills a two-run home run in the first inning. *AP Photo*

HOUSTON -- Carlos Correa homered, doubled and drove in four runs, Jose Altuve got two more hits and the Houston Astros battered the Boston Red Sox 8-2 to take a commanding 2-0 lead in the AL Division Series.

George Springer also homered to back Dallas Keuchel in Houston's second straight romp by the exact same score.

"One through nine, everybody can do damage, everybody can go deep," Correa said. "That's the good thing about our

Starting pitcher Dallas Keuchel struck out seven while giving up only one earned run. *AP Photo*

lineup, there are no holes in our lineup, and we feel very confident no matter if we went 0 for 4 the day before or if we went 4 for 4."

A day after Altuve hit three home runs in the playoff opener, he got things going with a two-out single in the first inning off Drew Pomeranz. Correa, who went 0 for 4 in Game 1, made it 2-0 when he launched a towering shot onto the train tracks atop left field.

Keuchel pitched into the sixth, allowing one run and three hits while striking out seven to improve to 3-0 with a 0.96 ERA in three career postseason starts.

After Jackie Bradley Jr. had an RBI single in the Boston second, the Astros started to break away.

Springer hit his first postseason homer when he sent the second pitch of the third inning into the front row of the seats in right field.

A double by Alex Bregman set up an RBI single by Altuve later in the third, making it 4-1 and ending Pomeranz's first career postseason start after two relief appearances. The lefty kept his head down as he trudged toward the dugout after being lifted.

"Any mistake that we've made these past two games, they've made us pay for them," Pomeranz said. "It's playoff baseball, and these guys have come out swinging."

David Price, the starter-turned-reliever with the $217 million contract, pitched 2 2/3 scoreless innings for the Red Sox. Following his exit, Houston tacked on four runs in the sixth.

A two-out intentional walk to Altuve, the major league batting champion this season, led to a two-run double by Correa . The top overall pick in the 2012 draft and crown jewel of Houston's years long rebuilding project raised his hands in delight and motioned for the crowd to get louder as he stopped at second base.

Keuchel, the 2015 AL Cy Young Award winner, had trouble settling in early and after needing 30 pitches to get through the second inning, it looked like this start might be a short one. But he struck out the last two batters of that inning as the first of 13 straight he retired.

BOX SCORE

	1	2	3	4	5	6	7	8	9	R	H	E
BOS	0	1	0	0	0	0	0	0	1	2	7	1
HOU	2	0	2	0	0	4	0	0	-	8	12	0

RED SOX

HITTERS	AB	R	H	RBI	BB	K	AVG
X. Bogaerts-SS	5	0	0	0	0	2	.000
D. Pedroia-2B	3	0	1	0	1	1	.167
B. Holt-PR-2B	0	0	0	0	0	0	.000
A. Benintendi-LF	4	0	0	0	0	1	.125
M. Betts-RF	4	0	1	0	0	1	.375
R. Davis-RF	0	0	0	0	0	0	.000
H. Ramirez-1B	3	0	0	0	1	2	.333
C. Young-DH	2	1	1	0	0	0	.500
M. Moreland-PH-DH	2	0	0	0	0	0	.200
C. Vazquez-C	3	1	2	0	1	1	.667
D. Marrero-3B	2	0	0	0	0	2	.000
R. Devers-PH-3B	2	0	0	0	0	1	.000
J. Bradley Jr.-CF	4	0	2	2	0	0	.286
TEAM	**34**	**2**	**7**	**2**	**3**	**11**	

ASTROS

HITTERS	AB	R	H	RBI	BB	K	AVG
G. Springer-CF-RF	4	2	2	1	1	0	.250
A. Bregman-3B	5	1	1	0	0	0	.333
J. Altuve-2B	3	2	2	1	2	1	.714
C. Correa-SS	4	2	2	4	1	0	.250
E. Gattis-DH	3	0	1	1	1	1	.500
C. Beltran-PH	1	0	1	0	0	0	1.000
D. Fisher-PR-DH	0	0	0	0	0	0	.000
J. Reddick-RF	4	0	0	0	0	1	.286
C. Maybin-PH-CF	1	0	0	0	0	0	.000
Y. Gurriel-1B	4	0	1	0	1	1	.250
M. Gonzalez-LF	4	1	1	0	0	1	.250
B. McCann-C	3	0	1	0	0	0	.250
TEAM	**36**	**8**	**12**	**7**	**6**	**5**	

RED SOXS

PITCHERS	IP	H	R	ER	BB	K	HR	ERA
D. Pomeranz (L, 0-1)	2.0	5	4	4	1	1	2	18.00
C. Smith	0.1	0	0	0	2	0	0	0.00
D. Price	2.2	1	0	0	1	2	0	0.00
E. Rodriguez	0.0	1	2	2	0	0	0	INF
A. Reed	1.0	2	2	2	1	0	0	18.00
A. Maddox	1.0	2	0	0	1	1	0	4.50
C. Kimbrel	1.0	1	0	0	0	1	0	0.00
TEAM	8.0	12	8	8	6	5	2	

ASTROS

PITCHERS	IP	H	R	ER	BB	K	HR	ERA
D. Keuchel (W, 1-0)	5.2	3	1	1	3	7	0	1.59
C. Devenski (H, 1)	1.1	1	0	0	0	1	0	0.00
L. Gregerson	1.0	1	0	0	0	2	0	0.00
K. Giles	1.0	2	1	1	0	1	0	9.00
TEAM	9.0	7	2	2	3	11	0	

Keuchel exited to a standing ovation after walking Hanley Ramirez with two outs in the sixth inning.

"We couldn't really script it any better," Keuchel said.

Boston Red Sox right fielder Mookie Betts robs the Astros Alex Bregman of extra-bases during the third inning of Game 3.
AP Photo

OCTOBER 8, 2017   FENWAY PARK   BOSTON, MASSACHUSETTS
HOUSTON ASTROS 3 • BOSTON RED SOX 10

Red Sox avoid ALDS elimination

Carlos Correa celebrates as he rounds the bases following his two-run home run in the first inning. *AP Photo*

BOSTON -- David Price pitched four scoreless innings of relief after another Boston starter faltered, and 20-year-old Rafael Devers connected for a key homer as the Red Sox beat the Houston Astros 10-3 to stave off elimination in Game 3 of the AL Division Series.

After losses in the first two games left the Red Sox hoping to avoid a sweep, Hanley Ramirez cheered up the Fenway Park crowd by waving a "Believe in Boston" flag during introductions. He then delivered four hits and three RBIs to help the Red Sox snap a five-game postseason losing streak.

"I just tried to wake everybody up," Ramirez said. "I think that's my job: Find a

53

Marwin Gonzalez right, exchanges words with Red Sox catcher Sandy Leon after striking out to end the top of the seventh inning. *AP Photo*

way to come through in big situations, It's the playoffs. It's go time."

Mitch Moreland had three hits and Jackie Bradley Jr. hit his first postseason homer, a three-run shot in a six-run seventh that helped Boston pull away.

After winning each of the first two games 8-2, Carlos Correa homered for the Astros as they took a first-inning lead for the third straight game. Up 3-0 with two on and one out in the second, Houston chased Doug Fister and Joe Kelly retired George Springer before Josh Reddickhit a long fly ball to right field that Mookie Betts caught at the top of the short wall to end the inning.

"It would have been a great spot for us to get another three runs and big momentum for us. And that seemed to be big momentum for those guys," Reddick said. "They come up after that and they take the lead. So I just wish the park was a little bit shorter."

Kelly pitched the third and then Price turned in his seventh straight scoreless appearance since going to the bullpen in September after missing most of the season with left elbow problems.

Astros starter Brad Peacock escaped the second inning with a 3-1 lead despite loading the bases with nobody out, but he ran into bigger trouble in the third.

After Peacock struck out Boston's No. 3 and 4 hitters, Andrew Benintendi and Mookie Betts, Moreland doubled and scored on Ramirez's line drive over left fielder Marwin Gonzalez's outstretched glove. Francisco Liriano gave up Devers' two-run homer to right that gave Boston a 4-3 lead - its first in 44 postseason innings dating to Game 1 of the 2016 ALDS.

Devers, who turns 21 on Oct. 24, is the youngest Red Sox player to homer in the postseason and one of only six players in major league history to hit a postseason home run before their 21st birthday.

Ramirez drove in two more runs in a six-run seventh inning highlighted by Bradley's homer that bounced off Reddick's glove and into the stands behind the Pesky Pole.

Price allowed four hits and a walk. He exchanged words with Gonzalez after

striking him out with a 95 mph fastball to end the seventh, and home plate umpire Ted Barrett walked toward the Red Sox dugout with catcher Sandy Leon to calm things down.

Peacock allowed three runs and six hits in 2 2/3 innings. Liriano got just one out while allowing one run and two hits for the Astros.

BOX SCORE

	1	2	3	4	5	6	7	8	9	R	H	E
HOU	3	0	0	0	0	0	0	0	0	3	13	2
BOS	0	1	3	0	0	0	6	0	-	10	15	0

ASTROS
HITTERS	AB	R	H	RBI	BB	K	AVG
G. Springer-CF	5	1	2	0	0	1	.308
J. Reddick-RF	5	1	2	1	0	0	.333
J. Altuve-2B	4	0	3	0	1	0	.727
C. Correa-SS	5	1	1	2	0	1	.231
M. Gonzalez-LF	4	0	1	0	0	2	.250
A. Bregman-3B	4	0	0	0	0	1	.231
C. Beltran-DH	3	0	0	0	1	1	.250
Y. Gurriel-1B	4	0	4	0	0	0	.500
B. McCann-C	4	0	0	0	0	0	.250
J. Centeno-C	0	0	0	0	0	0	.000
TEAM	**38**	**3**	**13**	**3**	**2**	**6**	

RED SOX
HITTERS	AB	R	H	RBI	BB	K	AVG
X. Bogaerts-SS	5	0	0	0	0	1	.000
D. Pedroia-2B	5	0	1	0	0	0	.182
A. Benintendi-LF	4	1	1	0	1	1	.167
M. Betts-RF	4	1	1	0	1	3	.333
M. Moreland-1B	5	3	3	0	0	1	.400
H. Ramirez-DH	4	2	4	3	0	0	.600
R. Devers-3B	3	2	2	3	1	0	.250
S. Leon-C	4	0	2	1	0	1	.500
J. Bradley Jr.-CF	4	1	1	3	0	2	.273
TEAM	**38**	**10**	**15**	**10**	**3**	**9**	

ASTROS
PITCHERS	IP	H	R	ER	BB	K	HR	ERA
B. Peacock	2.2	6	3	3	1	4	0	10.13
F. Liriano (L, 0-1)	0.1	2	1	1	0	0	1	13.50
L. McCullers Jr.	3.0	3	2	2	2	4	0	6.00
C. Devenski	0.0	3	3	3	0	0	0	11.57
J. Musgrove	1.0	1	1	1	0	0	1	4.50
L. Gregerson	1.0	0	0	0	0	1	0	0.00
TEAM	**8.0**	**15**	**10**	**10**	**3**	**9**	**2**	

RED SOXS
PITCHERS	IP	H	R	ER	BB	K	HR	ERA
D. Fister	1.1	4	3	3	1	1	1	20.25
J. Kelly (W, 1-0)	1.2	2	0	0	0	0	0	0.00
D. Price (H, 1)	4.0	4	0	0	1	4	0	0.00
A. Reed	1.0	1	0	0	0	0	0	9.00
C. Smith	1.0	2	0	0	0	1	0	0.00
TEAM	**9.0**	**13**	**3**	**3**	**2**	**6**	**1**	

Houston right fielder Josh Reddick delivers a huge RBI single in the ninth inning of Game 4. *AP Photo*

OCTOBER 9, 2017 FENWAY PARK BOSTON, MASSACHUSETTS

HOUSTON ASTROS 5 • BOSTON RED SOX 4

Astros advance to ALCS

Houston Astros manager A.J. Hinch, third from left, gives the ball to pitcher Justin Verlander for his very first Major League relief appearance during the fifth inning. *AP Photo*

BOSTON -- The Houston Astros poured back onto the field after advancing to their first AL Championship Series, posing for pictures with the Green Monster as a backdrop before a few players bellyflopped in the puddles in the infield dirt.

"Both teams were throwing their guys, and that's what you live for," Houston third baseman Alex Bregman said after Justin Verlander came out of the bullpen to beat Chris Sale in an aces-turned-relievers role reversal and helped the Astros eliminate the Red Sox in four games with a 5-4 victory.

Houston players celebrate following their 5-4 ALDS clinching win over Boston. *AP Photo*

"When we saw Verlander run to the `pen we said, `Our horse is on the mound, we need to win this game," said Bregman, who homered off Sale to tie it in the eighth before Josh Reddick's single gave the Astros the lead. "That's kind of the whole energy that he's brought here. He's brought an energy with him that, `Hey, when he's out there, we're going to win."

Verlander, who was acquired for the playoff run after spending his first 13 seasons in Detroit, gave up the go-ahead homer to Andrew Benintendi -- the first batter he faced -- before shutting Boston down for the next 2 2/3 innings.

The former AL MVP and Cy Young winner earned the victory in his first relief appearance after 424 starts in a major and minor league career.

"All the things that you would like to do as a starter, I was able to do that,"

Verlander said. "Top to bottom, man, these guys grinded against two of the toughest competitors in this game in Sale and (closer Craig) Kimbrel."

The Red Sox forced a Game 4 after losing the first two games in Houston, and then took a 3-2 lead in the fifth on Benintendi's homer. Bregman tied it before Reddick's single off closer Craig Kimbrel made it 4-3.

Carlos Beltran added to his postseason legacy with an RBI double in the ninth -- an insurance run that became the game-winner when Rafael Devers hit an inside-the-park homer off closer Ken Giles over leaping center fielder George Springer and off the Green Monster toward center.

The 20-year-old Red Sox rookie easily circled the bases before the throw to make it 5-4.

Giles retired the next three batters for the six-out save.

"The two big boys, Sale and Verlander, both get into the game. Everybody did well," Houston manager A.J. Hinch said. "Nobody really wanted to concede the game."

The Astros last reached the league championship series in 2005 as a National League team, and were swept in the World Series by the White Sox. This year's team, wearing "Houston Strong" patches to support the city that was flooded in Hurricane Harvey, is hoping to finish the job.

"The city of Houston is still rebuilding," Hinch said. "It's easy for us to look in the rearview mirror and think that the hurricane is over (but) the rebuild is not going to stop for a long time. ... We want to win for them, we want to win for us, we want to win because we showed up in spring training to try to win a World Series."

BOX SCORE

	1	2	3	4	5	6	7	8	9	R	H	E
HOU	1	1	0	0	0	0	2	1		5	12	0
BOS	1	0	0	0	2	0	0	0	1	4	9	1

ASTROS

HITTERS	AB	R	H	RBI	BB	K	AVG
G. Springer-CF	4	1	3	1	1	0	.412
J. Reddick-RF	4	0	2	1	1	0	.375
J. Altuve-2B	4	0	0	0	1	1	.533
C. Correa-SS	4	0	1	0	1	3	.235
M. Gonzalez-LF	3	1	0	0	0	1	.200
A. Bregman-3B	5	1	1	1	0	1	.222
Y. Gurriel-1B	5	1	3	0	0	0	.529
E. Gattis-DH	4	0	1	0	0	2	.400
C. Maybin-PR-DH	0	1	0	0	0	0	.000
C. Beltran-PH-DH	1	0	1	1	0	0	.400
B. McCann-C	5	0	0	0	0	3	.125
TEAM	**39**	**5**	**12**	**4**	**4**	**11**	

RED SOX

HITTERS	AB	R	H	RBI	BB	K	AVG
D. Pedroia-2B	5	0	0	0	0	1	.125
X. Bogaerts-SS	3	2	1	1	1	0	.059
A. Benintendi-LF	4	1	2	2	0	0	.250
M. Betts-RF	4	0	1	0	0	0	.313
M. Moreland-1B	3	0	1	0	1	1	.385
H. Ramirez-DH	4	0	2	0	0	0	.571
R. Devers-3B	3	1	2	1	1	1	.364
C. Vazquez-C	3	0	0	0	1	1	.333
J. Bradley Jr.-CF	4	0	0	0	0	3	.200
TEAM	**33**	**4**	**9**	**4**	**4**	**7**	

ASTROS

PITCHERS	IP	H	R	ER	BB	K	HR	ERA
C. Morton	4.1	7	2	2	6	1		4.15
J. Verlander (W, 2-0)	2.2	1	1	1	2	0	1	3.12
K. Giles (S, 1)	2.0	1	1	1	0	1	1	6.00
TEAM	**9.0**	**9**	**4**	**4**	**4**	**7**	**3**	

RED SOXS

PITCHERS	IP	H	R	ER	BB	K	HR	ERA
R. Porcello	3.0	5	2	2	3	4	0	4.50
C. Sale (L, 0-2)	4.2	4	2	2	0	6	1	8.38
C. Kimbrel	1.0	3	1	1	1	1	0	4.50
A. Reed	0.1	0	0	0	0	0	0	7.71
TEAM	**9.0**	**12**	**5**	**5**	**4**	**11**	**1**	

ASTROS FEATURE
JOSE ALTUVE & CARLOS CORREA

A Brotherhood

Jose Altuve and Carlos Correa joke around during a workout prior to the World Series. *AP Photo*

The image from the pennant-trophy presentation neatly captured the Jose Altuve-Carlos Correa dynamic.

On the stage during the on-field ceremonies after the Houston Astros claimed the American League championship, both middle infielders wore expressions of satisfaction as the 6-4 Correa draped his arm over the shoulder of the 5-6 Altuve. They looked like brothers whose parents were about to reward them for a good deed.

Their positions on the field bring them together, as do their spots in the lineup as the No. 3 and 4 hitters in Houston's potent attack. But it's their mutual affinity off the field that forms the strongest bond. It may not be true that Altuve and Correa are inseparable, but it takes some effort to pry them apart.

"This team gets along very well. We have very good chemistry," Altuve said on the eve of Game 1 of the World Series, pitting the Astros against the Los Angeles Dodgers. "But Carlos and I have a little extra. I don't know if it's because we're a shortstop and a second baseman or

Carlos Correa congratulates Jose Altuve after hitting a home run. AP Photo

because we're both Latin guys, but it's really a very good relationship.''

It began in the spring trainings before Correa reached the majors in 2015 as a former No. 1 overall draft pick out of Puerto Rico. The Venezuelan-born Altuve, who had broken in in 2011, showed the heralded prospect the ropes, where to go, how to behave in a major league clubhouse.

Their partnership has helped lift an Astros team that lost 111 games as recently as 2013 to two playoff berths in the last three years and the franchise's second World Series appearance since its inception in 1962.

As a second baseman, Altuve has always made a point of establishing a rapport with his double-play partner that goes beyond their play around second base.

"But he and Correa take it to another level," Astros general manager Jeff Luhnow said. "They can almost anticipate each other's moves, which allows them to do things other combinations aren't able to do. It's like watching art unfold before your eyes."

Besides anchoring the infield at positions that traditionally oriented toward fielding, Altuve and Correa form the nucleus of an offense that scored the most runs in the big leagues.

Altuve, 27, just won his third batting title with a .346 average and led the AL in hits for a fourth year in a row while finishing third in the league in on-base plus slugging percentage at .957, tops among major league second basemen.

Correa, 23, missed 42 games with a thumb injury but still set career highs with 24 home runs and a .941 OPS, the highest of any shortstop.

No other second base-shortstop combination had both players with an OPS of .900 or above. The Indians' Jose Ramirez (.957) and Francisco Lindor (.842) came closest.

"Throughout the history of baseball, middle infield is one of those positions where you haven't always had to hit really well. You can get by with your glove," Astros pitcher Collin McHugh said. "But they've come to the forefront as middle infielders who are maybe bat-first. Not so say their defense isn't spectacular. They're probably going to have multiple Gold Gloves by the end of their careers. But what they're able to do offensively sets them apart from everybody else."

And, as often happens in brotherly-type relationships, they push each other to succeed. Correa, the 2015 AL rookie of the year, finds inspiration

in Altuve's persistent desire to improve.

After overcoming the bias he frequently encountered because of his stature, Altuve made the All-Star team in his first full season of 2012, when he batted .290 with a .740 OPS for a last-place team that lost 107 games. But when he got caught stealing a league-high 13 times in 2013, Altuve decided to focus on his baserunning the next season and led the AL with 56 steals while batting .341.

The next year he wanted to improve his fielding and wound up winning the Gold Glove. In the last two seasons, Altuve has made more of an effort to drive the ball while adding a leg kick. That paid off in back-to-back seasons of 24 homers and more than 81 RBI.

"He's never pleased," said Correa, who views Altuve as an older brother. "If he gets three hits in a game, he wants four. He has four and wants five. That impresses me."

Even though some metrics rank Correa as merely a slightly above-average defensive shortstop, Altuve often calls him the best player in baseball. Certainly, few possess his combination of athleticism and canon arm, let alone the offensive prowess.

In addition, Correa has long displayed maturity beyond his years, one of the reasons the Astros were so taken with him when deciding whom to choose with the top pick in the 2012 draft.

"I think at least 100 of the 200 hits I had this year were because of Carlos," Altuve said. "He would come up to me in the on-deck circle and say, 'Hey, this guy throws this stuff, try to do this.' So I would do that and get a hit. On that hit I got against Severino with the bases full, he gave me some encouragement and told me, 'Let's go. You're the one to deliver this hit.' That meant a lot to me. I went up to home plate and got the hit."

Yuli Gurriel hits an RBI single during the fourth inning of Game 1. *AP Photo*

OCTOBER 13, 2017   MINUTE MAID PARK   HOUSTON, TEXAS
HOUSTON ASTROS 2 • NEW YORK YANKEES 1

Keuchel shuts down Yankees

Houston starting pitcher Dallas Keuchel throws during the first inning of Game 1. *AP Photo*

HOUSTON -- Dallas Keuchel faced the New York Yankees in the postseason for the second time and the Houston Astros ace shut them down again.

Keuchel struck out 10 in seven scoreless innings to help Houston to a 2-1 victory on Friday night in the AL Championship Series opener.

"I think it's just pitch execution, and it's just been there more times than it hasn't against the Yankees," Keuchel said.

Keuchel threw six scoreless innings in a 3-0 win over New York in the 2015 AL wild card game.

He allowed four hits -- all singles -- and walked one to improve to 8-2 with

Houston catcher Brian McCann tags out the Yankees' Greg Bird at home after a perfect throw from left fielder Marwin Gonzalez during the fifth inning of Game 1. *AP Photo*

a 1.09 ERA in eight starts against the Yankees in the regular season and postseason combined. He joined Nolan Ryan and Mike Scott as the only Astros pitchers to reach double digits in strikeouts in a postseason game.

"Late movement -- he moves the ball and he commands it well," the Yankees Greg Bird said.

Carlos Correa and Yuli Gurriel hit RBI singles in the fourth off loser Masahiro Tanaka, and left fielder Marwin Gonzalez threw out Bird at the plate trying to score on Aaron Judge's two-out single in the fifth.

"We had a shot," Yankees manager Joe Girardi said. "If Bird's safe maybe we really get to him in that inning."

Bird homered off Ken Giles with two outs in the ninth, and the closer struck out pinch-hitter Jacoby Ellsbury. Giles, who threw a season-high 37 pitches, escaped a two-out jam in the eighth by striking out Didi Gregorius.

Greeted by MVP chants each time to the plate, Jose Altuve had three more hits and at 11 for 19 (.579) has the most hits in a team's first five postseason games since Seattle's Ichiro Suzuki in 2001.

After the Astros totaled eight runs in the first innings of their four AL Division Series games, Tanaka kept the Astros hitless until Altuve's infield single rolled through the pitcher's legs in the fourth. Altuve swiped second before scoring on Correa's single.

Gurriel followed with a two-out single, his 10th hit of the postseason.

Bird singled to start the fifth and Matt Holliday, making his first appearance of the postseason, reached when Altuve dropped his slow bouncer to second for an error. Judge singled with two outs and Gonzalez, throwing with such force that he fell to the ground, made a 97 mph one-hop throw to catcher Brian McCann, who tagged the sliding Bird.

"That was their best moment in the game, (I needed) to stop the momentum," Gonzalez said. "All I was thinking was to go get the ball as fast as I could."

The call was confirmed in a video review.

"I'm too slow. I wish I was a little faster," Bird said.

BOX SCORE

	1	2	3	4	5	6	7	8	9	R	H	E
NYY	0	0	0	0	0	0	0	0	1	1	5	0
HOU	0	0	0	2	0	0	0	0	-	2	6	1

YANKEES

HITTERS	AB	R	H	RBI	BB	K	AVG
B. Gardner-LF	3	0	1	0	1	2	.333
A. Judge-RF	3	0	1	0	1	1	.333
G. Sanchez-C	3	0	0	0	1	3	.000
R. Torreyes-PR	0	0	0	0	0	0	.000
A. Romine-C	0	0	0	0	0	0	.000
D. Gregorius-SS	4	0	0	0	0	2	.000
S. Castro-2B	4	0	1	0	0	1	.250
A. Hicks-CF	4	0	0	0	0	2	.000
G. Bird-1B	4	1	2	1	0	2	.500
M. Holliday-DH	3	0	0	0	0	0	.000
J. Ellsbury-PH	1	0	0	0	0	1	.000
T. Frazier-3B	3	0	0	0	0	0	.000
TEAM	**32**	**1**	**5**	**1**	**3**	**14**	

ASTROS

HITTERS	AB	R	H	RBI	BB	K	AVG
G. Springer-CF	3	0	0	0	1	2	.000
J. Reddick-RF	4	0	0	0	0	1	.000
J. Altuve-2B	4	1	3	0	0	0	.750
C. Correa-SS	4	1	1	1	0	1	.250
M. Gonzalez-LF	3	0	0	0	0	0	.000
Y. Gurriel-1B	3	0	1	1	0	0	.333
C. Beltran-DH	3	0	0	0	0	0	.000
A. Bregman-3B	3	0	1	0	0	0	.333
B. McCann-C	3	0	0	0	0	1	.000
TEAM	**30**	**2**	**6**	**2**	**1**	**5**	

YANKEES

PITCHERS	IP	H	R	ER	BB	K	HR	ERA
M. TANAKA (L, 0-1)	6.0	4	2	2	1	3	0	3.00
C. GREEN	2.0	2	0	0	0	2	0	0.00
TEAM	**8.0**	**6**	**2**	**2**	**1**	**5**	**0**	

ASTROS

PITCHERS	IP	H	R	ER	BB	K	HR	ERA
D. Keuchel (W, 1-0)	7.0	4	0	0	1	10	0	0.00
C. Devenski (H, 1)	0.1	0	0	0	1	0	0	0.00
K. Giles (S, 1)	1.2	1	1	1	1	4	1	5.40
TEAM	**9.0**	**5**	**1**	**1**	**3**	**14**	**1**	

Primarily an infielder, Gonzalez had just two outfield assists in the regular season. He beat his hand into his glove three times in celebration after watching McCann make the tag.

"It's one of the best throws I've ever seen from an outfielder," Correa said. "It was just perfect."

Houston Astros right fielder Josh Reddick makes a leaping catch before crashing into the wall in right field to rob the Yankees' Chase Headley of a hit. *AP Photo*

OCTOBER 14, 2017   MINUTE MAID PARK   HOUSTON, TEXAS
HOUSTON ASTROS 2 • NEW YORK YANKEES 1

Altuve, Verlander lift Astros to 2-0 lead

Jose Altuve slides in with the game-winning run as teammate Yuli Gurriel and the Houston fans celebrate. AP Photo

HOUSTON -- Jose Altuve and Justin Verlander. Houston's longest tenured player and its durable new ace have been an incomparable pair so far this postseason.

Altuve raced home on Carlos Correa's double in the ninth inning, Verlander struck out 13 in a complete game and the Astros beat the New York Yankees 2-1 for a 2-0 lead in the AL Championship Series.

Correa also homered, but Houston needed a daring dash from the 5-foot-

Starting pitcher Justin Verlander pitched a complete game while striking out 13. *AP Photo*

6 Altuve to get Verlander a win. Altuve, an AL MVP front-runner, reached with a one-out single against closer Aroldis Chapman, then sprinted around from first base on Correa's shot to right-center field. Shortstop Didi Gregorius' relay beat Altuve to the plate, but catcher Gary Sanchez misplayed a short-hop, allowing Houston's dynamo second baseman to slide past safely.

"When I saw him running I was like, `Oh God," Correa said. "And then obviously he beat it out."

Altuve had two more hits and is 13 for 23 (.565) this postseason after hitting just 4 for 26 (.154) in the 2015 playoffs.

"He's unbelievable," Verlander said. "The guy does everything."

Verlander improved to 8-0 in eight appearances with Houston since agreeing

to an Aug. 31 trade from the Tigers, including his Game 4 win in relief during a Division Series against Boston. He has a 2.04 ERA over a postseason-leading 17 2/3 innings.

"When I decided to say yes, these are the moments that you envision," Verlander said of agreeing to the trade. "You don't envision going 5-0 in the regular season once you get here, that's all fine and great, but that's not why I was brought here. I was brought here to help this team win a championship."

Verlander set a postseason career best for strikeouts and allowed five hits in his second career complete game in the playoffs. He threw a season-high 124 pitches and retired baby Bronx Bombers Aaron Judge, Sanchez and Greg Bird in the top of the ninth.

"This is such a big moment for our team, but he put us on his back today with his pitching," manager A.J. Hinch said.

Houston took its first ever 2-0 lead in a Championship Series in front of a crowd of 43,193 which included Houston Rockets stars James Harden, Chris Paul and Trevor Ariza in front-row seats. Minute Maid Park buzzed throughout, and fans let out huge cheers when Hinch sent Verlander back out to pitch the ninth.

"No words were necessary," Verlander said. "It was my game to win or lose."

Verlander got the first complete game by any pitcher this reliever-heavy postseason. The unshakable right-hander struck out the side in the eighth, and television shots showed fiance Kate

Upton in a pink sequined shirt cheering and clapping wildly as he walked off.

Verlander, Keuchel and two relievers have combined to strike out 27 Yankees in the series.

"They're making pitches on these kids," New York manager Joe Girardi said. "And maybe are they trying a little bit too hard? But I think everyone out there's probably trying a little bit too hard."

BOX SCORE

	1	2	3	4	5	6	7	8	9	R	H	E
NYY	0	0	0	0	1	0	0	0	0	1	5	0
HOU	0	0	0	1	0	0	0	0	1	2	5	0

YANKEES

HITTERS	AB	R	H	RBI	BB	K	AVG
B. Gardner-LF	4	0	1	0	0	3	.286
A. Judge-RF	4	0	0	0	0	2	.143
D. Gregorius-SS	4	0	1	0	0	0	.125
G. Sanchez-C	4	0	0	0	0	2	.000
G. Bird-1B	3	0	0	0	1	1	.286
S. Castro-2B	3	0	1	0	0	2	.286
A. Hicks-CF	3	1	1	0	0	1	.143
T. Frazier-3B	3	0	1	1	0	1	.167
C. Headley-DH	3	0	0	0	0	1	.000
TEAM	**31**	**1**	**5**	**1**	**1**	**13**	

ASTROS

HITTERS	AB	R	H	RBI	BB	K	AVG
G. Springer-CF	4	0	0	0	0	0	.000
J. Reddick-RF	4	0	0	0	0	1	.000
J. Altuve-2B	4	1	2	0	0	1	.625
C. Correa-SS	3	1	2	2	1	0	.429
M. Gonzalez-LF	3	0	0	0	0	1	.000
Y. Gurriel-1B	2	0	1	0	1	0	.400
C. Beltran-DH	3	0	0	0	0	0	.000
A. Bregman-3B	2	0	0	0	1	0	.200
B. McCann-C	3	0	0	0	0	1	.000
TEAM	**28**	**2**	**5**	**2**	**3**	**4**	

YANKEES

PITCHERS	IP	H	R	ER	BB	K	HR	ERA
L. SEVERINO	4.0	2	1	1	2	0	1	2.25
T. KAHNLE	2.0	0	0	0	1	1	0	0.00
D. ROBERTSON	2.0	1	0	0	0	2	0	0.00
A. CHAPMAN (L, 0-1)	0.1	2	1	1	0	1	0	27.00
TEAM	**8.1**	**5**	**2**	**2**	**3**	**4**	**1**	

ASTROS

PITCHERS	IP	H	R	ER	BB	K	HR	ERA
J. Verlander (W, 1-0)	9.0	5	1	1	1	13	0	1.00
TEAM	**9.0**	**5**	**1**	**1**	**3**	**14**	**1**	

Yankees right fielder Aaron Judge robs Astros designated hitter Yuli Gurriel of a home run during the fourth inning. *AP Photo*

OCTOBER 16, 2017   YANKEE STADIUM   NEW YORK, NEW YORK
HOUSTON ASTROS 1 • NEW YORK YANKEES 8

Judge, Sabathia lead Yankees to Game 3 win

The Yankees Aaron Judge hits a three-run home run during the fourth inning of Game 3. *AP Photo*

NEW YORK -- Back in the Bronx, the big guys delivered.

Aaron Judge hit a three-run homer and made a pair of sparkling catches helping to lead starting pitcher CC Sabathia and the New York Yankees over the Houston Astros 8-1 and cutting their deficit to 2-1 in the AL Championship Series.

Todd Frazier hit a go-ahead, three-run homer into the short porch in right field in the second inning against Charlie Morton.

The 6-foot-7 Judge entered in a 4-for-31 (.129) postseason slump that included one home run, four RBI and 19

Astros reliever Will Harris stretches for the throw to get Yankees shortstop Didi Gregorius by half a step. *AP Photo*

strikeouts. The slugger capped a five-run fourth with a laser of a drive to left field off Will Harris and robbed Yuli Gurriel and Cameron Maybin of extra-base hits.

Sabathia, almost as big at 6-foot-6, allowed three hits over six scoreless innings for his first postseason win in five years. After a pair of 2-1 losses in Houston, the Yankees led 8-0 after four innings.

New York improved to 4-0 at home this postseason. The Yankees were an AL-best 51-30 at home this season.

"We're somewhat built for this ballpark," manager Joe Girardi said.

Houston scored on a bases-loaded walk in the ninth before postseason star Jose Altuve grounded into a game-ending double

play with the bases loaded.

On the first chilly night of the autumn with a game-time temperature of 57, Sabathia relied on the sharp, slow slider that has helped revive the former flamethrower's career.

Pitching with caution to Houston's dangerous lineup, he walked four, struck out five and pitched shutout ball for the first time in 21 career postseason starts.

Houston loaded the bases with two outs in the third on a pair of two-out walks around Alex Bregman's single. But Carlos Correa popped out on a fastball in on his fists.

"I know he likes to get his hands extended," Sabathia said.

Judge used his height and long left arm to make a leaping catch with his left shoulder slamming into the right-field wall against Gurriel starting the fourth.

Then in the fifth, he sprinted into short right for a diving backhand catch on Maybin.

New York broke open the game in the bottom half. Chase Headley hit a run-scoring infield single -- ending an 0-for-28 slide by New York designated hitters in the postseason. Brett Gardner was hit on a leg by a pitch, loading the bases, and Astros reliever Will Harris came in and threw a wild pitch that allowed Frazier to come home from third.

"Judge did what Judge has done 50-plus times, which is hit the ball out of the ballpark when he gets a pitch to hit," Astros manager A.J. Hinch said.

BOX SCORE

	1	2	3	4	5	6	7	8	9	R	H	E
HOU	0	0	0	0	0	0	0	0	1	1	4	0
NYY	0	3	0	5	0	0	0	-		8	7	1

ASTROS

HITTERS	AB	R	H	RBI	BB	K	AVG
G. Springer-CF	4	0	1	0	1	2	.091
A. Bregman-3B	4	0	1	1	1	1	.222
J. Altuve-2B	4	0	0	0	1	1	.417
C. Correa-SS	4	0	1	0	0	1	.364
Y. Gurriel-DH	4	0	0	0	0	1	.222
E. Gattis-C	3	0	0	0	1	0	.000
M. Gonzalez-1B	3	1	0	0	1	1	.000
J. Reddick-RF	2	0	0	0	1	0	.000
D. Fisher-PH	0	0	0	0	1	0	.000
C. Maybin-LF	3	0	1	0	1	0	.333
TEAM	**31**	**1**	**4**	**1**	**8**	**7**	

YANKEES

HITTERS	AB	R	H	RBI	BB	K	AVG
B. Gardner-LF	3	1	0	0	0	1	.200
A. Judge-RF	3	1	1	3	1	2	.200
D. Gregorius-SS	4	0	1	0	0	0	.167
G. Sanchez-C	4	0	0	0	0	0	.000
G. Bird-1B	3	1	1	0	1	1	.300
S. Castro-2B	4	1	1	0	0	1	.273
A. Hicks-CF	4	1	1	0	0	0	.182
T. Frazier-3B	2	2	1	3	1	0	.250
C. Headley-DH	3	1	1	1	0	1	.167
TEAM	**30**	**8**	**7**	**7**	**3**	**6**	

ASTROS

PITCHERS	IP	H	R	ER	BB	K	HR	ERA
C. MORTON (L, 0-1)	3.2	6	7	7	2	3	1	17.18
W. HARRIS	0.1	1	1	1	0	0	1	27.00
C. MCHUGH	4.0	0	0	0	1	3	0	0.00
TEAM	**8.0**	**7**	**8**	**8**	**3**	**6**	**2**	

YANKEES

PITCHERS	IP	H	R	ER	BB	K	HR	ERA
C. Sabathia (W, 1-0)	6.0	3	0	0	4	5	0	0.00
A. Warren	2.0	0	0	0	1	1	0	0.00
D. Betances	0.0	0	1	1	2	0	0	INF
T. Kahnle	1.0	1	0	0	1	1	0	0.00
TEAM	**9.0**	**4**	**1**	**1**	**8**	**7**	**0**	

Yankees right fielder Aaron Judge reacts after hitting an RBI double during the eight inning as second baseman Jose Altuve looks on.   *AP Photo*

OCTOBER 17, 2017   YANKEE STADIUM   NEW YORK, NEW YORK
HOUSTON ASTROS 4   •   NEW YORK YANKEES 6

Yankees rally to beat Astros, ALCS tied 2-2

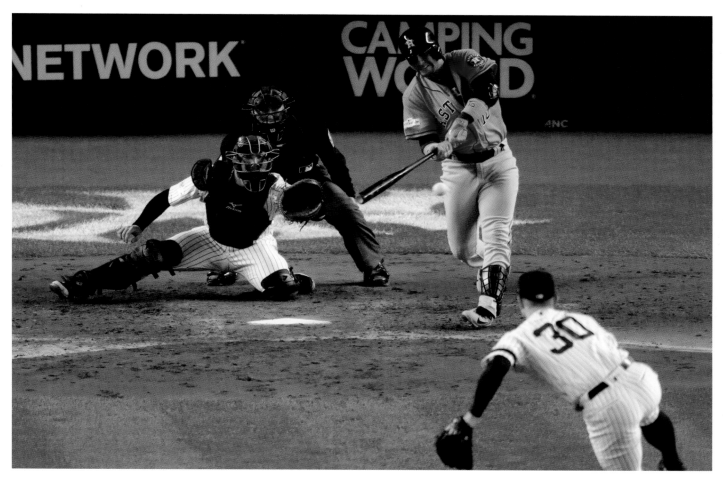

Yuli Gurriel delivers a big three-run double during the sixth inning. *AP Photo*

NEW YORK -- With a soaring shot headed for Monument Park, Aaron Judge got New York back on course for another memorable October.

Judge ignited a comeback with a home run, then hit a tying double during a four-run eighth inning to spur the unflappable Yankees over the Houston Astros 6-4 and tie the AL Championship Series 2-2.

The Baby Bombers trailed 4-0 against starter Lance McCullers Jr. until Judge homered leading off the seventh. The Yankees overcame three errors and have

Yankees shortstop Didi Gregorius leaps to catch a ball thrown in from the outfield following a second inning double by the Astros Carlos Beltran. *AP Photo*

roared back from a second straight 0-2 series deficit. New York improved to 5-0 at home in the playoffs and won for the 18th time in its last 21 home games.

"Every home game has been special," manager Joe Girardi said. "I just feel like the fans are back."

An AL MVP candidate mired in a sluggish October, Judge sparked the Yankees by chasing McCullers, who baffled the Yankees with his power breaking ball.

Except for the last one.

Judge launched a curveball into the netting above center field's Monument Park for New York's second hit.

Houston manager A.J. Hinch pulled McCullers after 81 pitches, Didi Gregorius tripled off Chris Devenski and Sanchez brought Gregorius in with a sacrifice fly.

Todd Frazier led off the eighth with a single to left, and pinch-hitter Chase

Headley singled. He lost his balance stepping on first, fell en route to second, then took a step back before continuing on and getting his left hand in ahead of Jose Altuve's tag.

Headley was awarded second after a video review, and the ballpark boomed when crew chief Gary Cederstrom gave the signal. Bret Gardner brought in Frazier on a groundout, and Judge came to bat with the bundled, buzzing crowd on its feet.

He lunged for a low slider and drilled a double high off the left-field wall as a fan in a longsleeve yellow shirt reached down and touched the ball. Pinch-runner Jacoby Ellsbury came home with the tying run, and Gregorius grounded a single just beyond shortstop Carlos Correa's reach to put runners at the corner. Sanchez, who had been 0 for 13 in the series, scored them both with a slicing drive that skipped to the wall in right-center.

Houston had not lost consecutive games since Sept. 8-10 at Oakland and had the major leagues' best road record during the regular season. The Astros are hitting .153 in the series.

"We're not going to hit the panic button because we lost two games in a row," Correa said. "We got Keuchel going tomorrow."

McCullers cruised in his first start since Sept. 30 and turned over a 4-1 lead to his bullpen.

"He was awesome," manager A.J. Hinch said. "I'm really proud of him because I know how important this start was for him."

Houston took a 3-0 lead in the sixth after George Springer walked leading off and Josh Reddick reached on catcher's interference by Austin Romine -- inserted into lineup for his defense.

Yuli Gurriel lined a three-run double off David Robertson for a 3-0 lead in the sixth and second baseman Starlin

BOX SCORE

	1	2	3	4	5	6	7	8	9	R	H	E
HOU	0	0	0	0	0	3	1	0	0	4	3	0
NYY	0	0	0	0	0	2	4	-		6	8	3

ASTROS

HITTERS	AB	R	H	RBI	BB	K	AVG
G. Springer-CF	3	1	0	0	1	0	.071
J. Reddick-RF	3	1	0	0	0	0	.000
J. Altuve-2B	2	1	0	0	2	1	.357
C. Correa-SS	4	0	0	0	0	2	.267
Y. Gurriel-1B	4	0	1	3	0	2	.231
A. Bregman-3B	4	0	0	0	0	1	.154
C. Beltran-DH	3	0	1	0	0	2	.111
E. Gattis-PH	1	0	0	0	0	0	.000
M. Gonzalez-LF	3	1	1	0	0	0	.083
B. McCann-C	2	0	0	0	0	1	.000
TEAM	**29**	**4**	**3**	**3**	**3**	**9**	

YANKEES

HITTERS	AB	R	H	RBI	BB	K	AVG
B. Gardner-LF	4	0	0	1	0	0	.143
A. Judge-RF	3	2	2	2	1	1	.308
D. Gregorius-SS	4	2	2	0	0	0	.250
G. Sanchez-C	3	0	1	3	0	0	.071
G. Bird-1B	1	0	0	0	3	1	.273
S. Castro-2B	3	0	0	0	1	0	.214
A. Hicks-CF	4	0	0	0	0	0	.133
T. Frazier-3B	4	1	2	0	0	1	.333
A. Romine-C	2	0	0	0	0	0	.000
C. Headley-PH	1	0	1	0	0	0	.286
J. Ellsbury-PR	0	1	0	0	0	0	.000
A. Chapman-P	0	0	0	0	0	0	.000
TEAM	**29**	**6**	**8**	**6**	**5**	**3**	

ASTROS

PITCHERS	IP	H	R	ER	BB	K	HR	ERA
L. MCCULLERS JR.	6.0	2	1	1	2	3	1	1.50
C. DEVENSKI (H, 2)	0.1	1	1	1	1	0	0	13.50
J. MUSGROVE (H, 1)	0.2	2	2	2	0	0	0	27.00
K. GILES (L, 0-1; B, 1)	0.1	3	2	2	1	0	0	13.50
L. GREGERSON	0.2	0	0	0	1	0	0	0.00
TEAM	**8.0**	**8**	**6**	**6**	**5**	**3**	**1**	

YANKEES

PITCHERS	IP	H	R	ER	BB	K	HR	ERA
S. Gray	5.0	1	2	1	2	4	0	1.80
D. Robertson	1.0	1	1	1	1	1	0	3.00
C. Green (W, 1-0)	2.0	1	1	0	0	2	0	0.00
A. Chapman (S, 1)	1.0	0	0	0	0	2	0	6.75
TEAM	**9.0**	**3**	**4**	**2**	**3**	**9**	**0**	

Castro misplayed Brian McCann's seventh-inning grounder for his second error, allowing Marwin Gonzalez to score from second.

Yankees starting pitcher Masahiro
Tanaka was dominant in Game 5
allowing just three hits through seven
innings. *AP Photo*

OCTOBER 18, 2017   YANKEE STADIUM   NEW YORK, NEW YORK
HOUSTON ASTROS 0 • NEW YORK YANKEES 5

Tanaka, Yankees put Astros on the brink

Jose Altuve and Carlos Correa watch from the dugout as Game 5 slips away. *AP Photo*

NEW YORK -- One more big win, and these Yankees are World Series-bound.

Masahiro Tanaka pitched seven innings of three-hit ball and New York finally solved a longtime nemesis at just the right moment, beating Dallas Keuchel and the Houston Astros 5-0 for a 3-2 lead in the AL Championship Series.

Gary Sanchez hit an RBI single off Keuchel and later homered to help the wild-card Yankees win for the third straight day at home.

To take the series, the Yankees knew they needed to win at least one game

Yankees left fielder Brett Gardner slides past Astros catcher Brian McCann to score during the third inning. *AP Photo*

started by Keuchel or Verlander, both Cy Young Award winners. Now they've done that -- and they don't want to let Houston back up.

Houston arrived up two games to none and appeared to be closing in on its second World Series appearance. But the Astros have been unable to put away these poised Yankees, who improved to 6-0 at home this postseason in front of their cheering, chanting fans.

"New York is no joke," Keuchel said afterward.

New York has won 19 of its past 22 games at Yankee Stadium.

Aaron Judge, Greg Bird and Didi Gregorius also delivered big hits as New

York chased Keuchel in the fifth and handed him his first postseason loss.

Keuchel had been Yankees kryptonite, entering 6-2 with a 1.09 ERA in eight career starts against New York -- including a pair of scoreless outings in playoff wins.

But this night belonged to Tanaka and the Baby Bombers.

New York finally broke through against Keuchel with two outs in the second, when Starlin Castro doubled and scored on Greg Bird's sharp single.

"The most frustrating part is the fact that I didn't pick the guys up and they were looking towards me to kind of saddle up and get this thing back going again," Keuchel said. "That's a talented

BOX SCORE

	1	2	3	4	5	6	7	8	9		R	H	E
HOU	0	0	0	0	0	0	0	0	0		0	4	1
NYY	0	1	1	0	1	0	1	0	-		5	10	1

ASTROS

HITTERS	AB	R	H	RBI	BB	K	AVG
G. Springer-CF	4	0	1	0	0	1	.111
J. Reddick-RF	4	0	0	0	0	2	.000
J. Altuve-2B	4	0	0	0	0	0	.278
C. Correa-SS	4	0	1	0	0	1	.263
Y. Gurriel-1B	4	0	1	0	0	1	.235
A. Bregman-3B	4	0	0	0	0	0	.118
C. Beltran-DH	3	0	0	0	0	2	.083
M. Gonzalez-LF	3	0	1	0	0	1	.133
B. McCann-C	2	0	0	0	1	1	.000
TEAM	**32**	**0**	**4**	**0**	**1**	**9**	

YANKEES

HITTERS	AB	R	H	RBI	BB	K	AVG
B. Gardner-LF	5	1	0	0	0	2	.105
A. Judge-RF	3	1	1	1	1	2	.313
G. Sanchez-C	4	1	2	2	0	2	.167
D. Gregorius-SS	4	0	2	1	0	2	.300
A. Hicks-CF	4	0	0	0	0	1	.105
S. Castro-2B	4	1	1	0	0	2	.222
G. Bird-1B	2	0	1	1	2	1	.308
T. Frazier-3B	4	0	0	0	0	1	.250
C. Headley-DH	4	1	3	0	0	0	.455
TEAM	**34**	**5**	**10**	**5**	**3**	**13**	

ASTROS

PITCHERS	IP	H	R	ER	BB	K	HR	ERA
D. KEUCHEL (L, 1-1)	4.2	7	4	4	1	8	0	3.09
W. HARRIS	1.0	1	0	0	1	1	0	6.75
B. PEACOCK	1.1	2	1	1	0	3	1	6.75
F. LIRIANO	1.0	0	0	0	1	1	0	0.00
TEAM	**8.0**	**10**	**5**	**5**	**3**	**13**	**1**	

YANKEES

PITCHERS	IP	H	R	ER	BB	K	HR	ERA
M. Tanaka (W, 1-1)	7.0	3	0	0	1	8	0	1.38
T. Kahnle	2.0	1	0	0	0	1	0	0.00
TEAM	**9.0**	**4**	**0**	**0**	**1**	**9**	**0**	

group over there and 1 through 9 right now the bats have woken up and it's quite a challenge."

In the third, Judge grounded an RBI double just inside the third base line and past a diving Alex Bregman. Brett Gardner sped all the way around from first and scored with a headfirst slide.

Bregman's throwing error on an infield single by Headley, who had three hits in the No. 9 spot, aided the Yankees in the fifth. Keuchel walked Judge with two outs before Sanchez lined a run-scoring single into the left-field corner.

Going into that at-bat, Sanchez was 1 for 16 with seven strikeouts in the series -- and 0 for 8 with six strikeouts against Keuchel overall.

Gregorius then grounded an RBI single up the middle that grazed the glove of diving second baseman Jose Altuve. That ended the night for Keuchel and gave the Yankees a 4-0 cushion, the most runs he had ever allowed against them.

"When you play at home, things like this happen and that's why it's so tough to win on the road in the playoffs," Keuchel said. "Yankee Stadium is a tough place to play and it was rockin' these three games, but it's going to be rockin' back in Houston for us."

Justin Verlander allowed only five hits in his seven innings of work. *AP Photo*

OCTOBER 20, 2017   MINUTE MAID PARK   HOUSTON, TEXAS
HOUSTON ASTROS 7 • NEW YORK YANKEES 1

JUSTIN TIME
Verlander, Astros force Game 7

Houston catcher Brian McCann hits an RBI double during the fifth inning of Game 6. *AP Photo*

HOUSTON -- Justin Verlander remained perfect with the Houston Astros when they couldn't afford anything else.

The ace right-hander pitched seven shutout innings and Jose Altuve homered and drove in three runs during a 7-1 victory over the New York Yankees that extended the AL Championship Series to a decisive Game 7.

"He's been everything that we could have hoped for and more," Astros manager A.J. Hinch said about Verlander. "He chose to come here for games like

Houston center fielder George Springer makes a great catch against the wall on a ball hit by the Yankees Todd Frazier during the seventh inning. Starting pitcher Justin Verlander (inset) congratulates him on the great play. *AP Photo*

this and beyond."

Acquired in an Aug. 31 trade, Verlander has won all nine of his outings for the Astros -- including three starts and his first career relief appearance during the postseason. With his new club facing playoff elimination for the first time in Game 6 against the Yankees, he delivered again to tie the series 3-all.

"There's no point in saving anything,"

Verlander said, acknowledging the last two innings took a lot out of him.

George Springer helped the 34-year-old Verlander out of a jam in the seventh, leaping to make a catch at the center-field wall that robbed Todd Frazier of extra bases with two on and the Astros up 3-0.

"I thought homer," Verlander said. "That was obviously one of the big turning moments in the game."

When it was over, Verlander had

improved to 4-1 with a 1.21 ERA in five career postseason elimination games. He ran his scoreless streak in such games to 24 innings.

"I literally love Justin Verlander," Altuve said. "The way he goes out there makes me feel like I have to go out there and play the same way he's doing it."

Brian McCann's RBI ground-rule double in the fifth ended an 0-for-20 slump before Altuve snapped an 0-for-12 skid with a two-run single later in the inning.

Altuve hit his fourth homer of the postseason when he connected on a solo shot off David Robertson in the eighth.

"I love the way we played today," Altuve said.

Judge cut the lead to 3-1 with a homer off Brad Peacock in the eighth. But Peacock settled down after the homer by Judge, retiring the next two batters, capped by a strikeout of Gary Sanchez to end the inning. Ken Giles finished it off with a scoreless ninth.

Houston led the majors in scoring during the regular season but had struggled in this series, managing just nine runs in the first five games. Alex Bregman belted a two-run double in the eighth to make it 6-1, giving the Astros more runs than they'd managed in their last three games.

Verlander knew Houston's powerful

offense would get going sooner or later. He's just glad it happened before it was too late.

"There was no question these guys were going to break out, it was just a matter of time," he said. "Thankfully that wasn't next year."

BOX SCORE

	1	2	3	4	5	6	7	8	9	R	H	E
NYY	0	0	0	0	0	0	0	1	0		1	7	1
HOU	0	0	0	0	3	0	0	4	-		7	8	0

YANKEES

HITTERS	AB	R	H	RBI	BB	K	AVG
B. Gardner-LF	4	0	1	0	0	0	.130
A. Judge-RF	4	1	1	1	0	2	.300
D. Gregorius-SS	4	0	1	0	0	0	.292
G. Sanchez-C	4	0	1	0	0	1	.182
G. Bird-1B	3	0	0	0	1	2	.250
S. Castro-2B	3	0	1	0	0	0	.238
A. Hicks-CF	3	0	0	0	1	3	.091
T. Frazier-3B	4	0	0	0	0	1	.200
C. Headley-DH	4	0	2	0	0	1	.467
TEAM	33	1	7	1	2	10	

ASTROS

HITTERS	AB	R	H	RBI	BB	K	AVG
G. Springer-CF	4	0	0	0	1	2	.091
J. Reddick-RF	4	0	0	0	0	1	.000
J. Altuve-2B	4	1	2	3	0	1	.318
C. Correa-SS	4	1	2	0	0	0	.304
Y. Gurriel-1B	3	1	1	0	1	0	.250
A. Bregman-3B	3	2	1	2	1	1	.150
M. Gonzalez-LF	3	0	0	0	1	1	.111
E. Gattis-DH	2	1	0	1	1	1	.000
B. McCann-C	4	1	2	1	0	0	.143
TEAM	31	7	8	7	5	7	

YANKEES

PITCHERS	IP	H	R	ER	BB	K	HR	ERA
L. SEVERINO (L, 0-1)	4.2	3	3	3	4	3	0	4.15
C. GREEN	2.1	0	0	0	1	3	0	0.00
D. ROBERTSON	0.0	4	4	4	0	0	1	15.00
D. BETANCES	1.0	1	0	0	0	1	0	9.00
TEAM	8.0	8	7	7	5	7	1	

ASTROS

PITCHERS	IP	H	R	ER	BB	K	HR	ERA
J. Verlander (W, 2-0)	7.0	5	0	0	1	8	0	0.56
B. Peacock (H, 1)	1.0	1	1	1	0	1	1	7.71
K. Giles	1.0	1	0	0	1	1	0	9.00
TEAM	9.0	7	1	1	2	10	1	

Jose Altuve and ALCS MVP Justin Verlander hug after winning Game 7. *AP Photo*

OCTOBER 21, 2017   MINUTE MAID PARK   HOUSTON, TEXAS
HOUSTON ASTROS 4 • NEW YORK YANKEES 0

World Series bound: 'This city, they deserve this'

Houston Astros players celebrate reaching the World Series. *AP Photo*

HOUSTON-- Jose Altuve embraced Justin Verlander as confetti rained down. An improbable thought just a few years ago, the Houston Astros are headed to the World Series.

Charlie Morton and Lance McCullers Jr. combined on a three-hitter, Altuve and Evan Gattis homered and the Astros reached the World Series for only the second time by blanking the New York Yankees 4-0 in Game 7 of the AL Championship Series.

"I love our personality," Astros manager A.J. Hinch said. "We have the right amount of fun, the right amount of seriousness, the right amount of

Houston Astros designated hitter Evan Gattis crushes a fourth inning home run. *AP Photo*

perspective when we need it. To win 100 games and still be hungry is pretty remarkable."

The Astros will try for their first World Series title, thanks in large part to Altuve, the diminutive second baseman who swings a potent bat, and Verlander, who switched teams for the first time in his career to chase a ring.

Four years removed from their third straight 100-loss season in 2013, the Astros shut down the Yankees on consecutive nights after dropping three in a row in the Bronx.

The only previous time the Astros made it this far, they were a National League team when they were swept by the Chicago White Sox in 2005.

Hinch's club has a chance to win that elusive first crown, while trying to boost a region still recovering from Hurricane Harvey.

"This city, they deserve this," McCullers said.

Clutch defensive plays by third baseman Alex Bregman and center fielder George Springer helped Houston improve to 6-0 at Minute Maid Park in these playoffs.

Morton bounced back from a loss in Game 3 to allow two hits over five scoreless innings. Starter-turned-postseason reliever McCullers limited the Yankees to just one hit while fanning six over the next four. A noted curveballer, McCullers finished up with 24 straight breaking pitches to earn his first major league save.

Combined, they throttled the wild-card Yankees one last time in Houston. Aaron Judge, Gary Sanchez and their New York teammates totaled just three runs in the four road games.

CC Sabathia entered 10-0 with a 1.69 ERA in 13 starts this season after a Yankees loss. But he struggled with command and was gone with one out in the fourth inning.

Houston was up 2-0 in fifth when former Yankees star Brian McCann came through for the second straight game by hitting a two-run double.

After going 0 for 5 with runners in scoring position through the first three innings, the Astros got on the board with no outs in the fourth with the 405-foot shot by Gattis.

Altuve launched a ball off Tommy Kahnle into the seats in right field with one out in the fifth for his fifth homer this postseason. It took a while for him to see that it was going to get out, and held onto his bat until he was halfway to first base before flipping it and trotting around the bases as chants of "MVP" rained down on him.

Carlos Correa and Yuli Gurriel hit consecutive singles before Kahnle struck out Gattis. McCann's two-strike double, which rolled into the corner of right field, cleared the bases to push the lead to 4-0.

BOX SCORE

	1	2	3	4	5	6	7	8	9	R	H	E
NYY	0	0	0	0	0	0	0	1	0	0	3	0
HOU	0	0	0	1	3	0	0	0	-	4	10	0

YANKEES

HITTERS	AB	R	H	RBI	BB	K	AVG
B. Gardner-LF	4	0	1	0	0	1	.148
A. Judge-RF	4	0	0	0	0	1	.250
D. Gregorius-SS	4	0	0	0	0	4	.250
G. Sanchez-C	4	0	1	0	0	1	.192
G. Bird-1B	4	0	1	0	0	0	.250
S. Castro-2B	3	0	0	0	0	2	.208
A. Hicks-CF	2	0	0	0	1	1	.083
T. Frazier-3B	2	0	0	0	1	0	.182
C. Headley-DH	3	0	0	0	0	1	.389
TEAM	30	0	3	0	2	11	

ASTROS

HITTERS	AB	R	H	RBI	BB	K	AVG
G. Springer-CF	4	0	1	0	0	0	.115
A. Bregman-3B	4	0	1	0	0	0	.167
J. Altuve-2B	3	1	1	1	1	1	.320
C. Correa-SS	4	1	2	0	0	0	.333
Y. Gurriel-1B	4	1	1	0	0	0	.250
E. Gattis-DH	4	1	1	1	0	1	.100
B. McCann-C	2	0	1	2	2	1	.188
M. Gonzalez-LF	4	0	1	0	0	0	.136
J. Reddick-RF	4	0	1	0	0	1	.040
TEAM	33	4	10	4	3	4	

YANKEES

PITCHERS	IP	H	R	ER	BB	K	HR	ERA
C. SABATHIA (L, 1-1)	3.1	5	1	1	3	0	1	0.96
T. KAHNLE	1.1	4	3	3	0	1	1	4.26
A. WARREN	1.1	0	0	0	0	0	0	0.00
D. ROBERTSON	2.0	1	0	0	0	3	0	9.00
TEAM	8.0	10	4	4	3	4	2	

ASTROS

PITCHERS	IP	H	R	ER	BB	K	HR	ERA
C. Morton (W, 1-1)	5.0	2	0	0	1	5	0	7.27
L. McCullers Jr. (S, 1)	4.0	1	0	0	1	6	0	0.90
TEAM	9.0	3	0	0	2	11	0	

"It's not easy to get here. And I don't take any of this for granted. And this is what we play for," Verlander said. "These are the experiences that you remember at the end of your career when you look back, winning these games, playing in the World Series. Hopefully, winning the World Series."

Houston catcher Brian McCann tags out the Yankees Greg Bird after receiving a perfect throw from third baseman Alex Bergman. McCann was able to hang onto the ball despite getting spiked in the forearm by Bird. *AP Photo*

Trade pays off for Verlander and Astros

Verlander does a pregame interview before taking the mound for the first time as an Astro. *AP Photo*

It was getting dangerously late, and the Detroit Tigers had little time to spare.

They had to talk to Justin Verlander.

And in a hurry.

The Tigers, after talking with the Houston Astros for nearly two months, finally got the deal they wanted.

Yet, there was less than an hour before the midnight ET trade deadline, and they still needed Verlander to sign off on the deal.

Verlander, who had full no-trade protection having spent at least 10 years in the big leagues and five with the same team, told the Tigers all along that if he was traded, his first choice was to the Los Angeles Dodgers. If that couldn't happen then his second choice was the Chicago Cubs. The Cubs wanted him, and were willing to assume most of Verlander's remaining contract, but simply didn't have the prospects to also include in a deal.

They were out.

Verlander was informed by the Tigers it would be the Astros or nobody.

So, after getting permission from the Tigers, he started making calls. The Astros called him. He had questions. Lots of them.

He talked with Astros ace Dallas Keuchel. He talked with Astros owner Jim Crane. He talked with Astros manager A.J. Hinch.

"He was a little worried about Houston (in the aftermath of Hurricane Harvey)," Crane said. "I told him, 'This town is going to be fine. It's going to take time. You will be received great here. We've got a good team, a good manager, a good front office. There won't be any problems here.

"The big thing to him was that he had never been traded. He didn't know a lot about the city. I told him, This is a great spot

Newly acquired pitcher Justin Verlander, center, shakes hands with manager A.J. Hinch, as general manager Jeff Lunhow, right, looks on.   *AP Photo*

of reaching your goal of winning the World Series. You got to take a shot.'

"He had to make up his mind in a hurry because there wasn't much time."

There was so little time that once the three Astros prospects cleared physicals - pitcher Franklin Perez, outfielder Daz Cameron and catcher Jake Rogers - Tigers GM Al Avila was waiting at Verlander's home with the trade papers for him to sign.

Verlander, once the Astros agreed to provide full no-trade rights while also voiding the 2020 option year in his contract, agreed about two minutes before midnight.

The two teams were ecstatic, celebrating late into the evening, and a city that has been devastated by one of the worst natural disasters in American history, received a jolt of energy.

"I think it will bring hope," Hinch said, "something to look forward to while we rebuild the city. I think this team will work really hard to make this city proud, make this city feel good when there are a lot of people going through tough times."

Verlander reminded the Astros that he's just as hungry as they are to make it happen. He has an MVP and Cy Young plaques in his trophy case, two no-hitters and two American League pennants, but not a World Series ring.

"He was so excited and he felt really good to join this type of contender," Hinch said. "He's been so successful in his career. The one thing missing was a World Series ring. He let it be known to me he wants to win, and he wants to win here. He respects the success we've had, and wants to do his part.

"We need to do everything we can to bring a winner to Houston."

Los Angeles ace Clayton
Kershaw struck out 11 in
Game 1. *AP Photo*

OCTOBER 24, 2017   DODGERS STADIUM   LOS ANGELES, CALIFORNIA
HOUSTON ASTROS 1 • LOS ANGELES DODGERS 3

Kershaw dominates World Series opener

Alex Bregman drills a fourth inning home run, one of only three hits given up by Dodgers starter Clayton Kershaw. *AP Photo*

LOS ANGELES -- If the Astros are going to deliver Houston its first World Series title the team will need to figure out how to score runs on the road, something it has struggled to do all postseason long.

Los Angeles Dodgers ace Clayton Kershaw delivered a signature performance, pitching the Dodgers past the Astros 3-1 in the World Series opener.

Boosted by Justin Turner's tiebreaking, two-run homer in the sixth inning off Astros starter Dallas Keuchel, Kershaw was in complete control against the highest-scoring team in the majors this season.

"I felt good. It's a tough lineup over there," Kershaw said. "They are a great fastball

Houston starting pitcher Dallas Keuchel reacts after giving up a two-run home run to the Dodgers Justin Turner during the sixth inning of Game 1. *AP Photo*

hitting team. You just have to make sure you don't make too many mistakes."

The left-hander had waited his whole career for this moment. And once he took the mound in his Series debut, he lived up every bit to the legacy of Sandy Koufax, Orel Hershiser and the greatest of Dodgers hurlers.

Astros manager A.J. Hinch downplayed the team's road struggles during a postgame press conference, instead pointing to the sensational performance by Kershaw.

"Tonight is about Kershaw," he said when asked about the Astros' inability to score runs on the road. "They had two big swings, we had one... It's no more complicated than that."

The three-time Cy Young Award winner struck out 11, gave up just three hits and walked none over seven innings, featuring a sharp breaking ball that often left Houston batters looking foolish. His lone blemish was a home run by Alex Bregman in the fourth that made it 1-all.

Brandon Morrow worked a perfect eighth and Kenley Jansen breezed through the Astros in the ninth for a save in a combined three-hitter. The Dodgers' dominant relievers have thrown 25 straight scoreless innings this postseason.

A pulsating crowd that came to see the Dodgers' first Series game since 1988 enjoyed an immediate jolt when Chris Taylor hit a no-doubt home run on Keuchel's very first pitch.

The lefthander recovered and completed 6 2/3 innings facing only one batter more than the minimum through five innings. He was backed by three double plays turned behind him.

A Series opener that served as a showcase for several of the game's best young hitters --Jose Altuve, Carlos Correa, Cody Bellinger and more -- instead was dominated by Kershaw.

Facing a team that had the fewest strikeouts in the majors this year, Kershaw fanned more Houston hitters than any starter this season adding to the offensive numbers for the Astros this postseason that are not pretty.

The Astros are a perfect 6-0 at home, but they are just 1-4 on the road, where they have plated an average of just 2.6 runs. To make matters worse, Houston pitchers have also struggled on the road, posting an ugly 7.24 ERA during away games compared to a 1.17

ERA at home.

The good news for the Astros is they will have ace Justin Verlander on the mound in Game 2.

The hard throwing right-hander is 4-0 with a 1.46 ERA in the postseason this year.

"It's a tough road when you go up against Kershaw," Hinch said. "But it's going to be a tough road when they go against Verlander."

BOX SCORE

	1	2	3	4	5	6	7	8	9	R	H	E
HOU	0	0	0	1	0	0	0	0	0	1	3	0
LAD	1	0	0	0	0	2	0	0	-	3	6	0

ASTROS

HITTERS	AB	R	H	RBI	BB	K	AVG
G. Springer-CF	4	0	0	0	0	4	.000
A. Bregman-3B	4	1	1	1	0	0	.250
J. Altuve-2B	4	0	1	0	0	1	.250
C. Correa-SS	3	0	0	0	0	1	.000
Y. Gurriel-1B	3	0	0	0	0	2	.000
B. McCann-C	3	0	0	0	0	0	.000
M. Gonzalez-LF	3	0	0	0	0	1	.000
J. Reddick-RF	3	0	1	0	0	1	.333
D. Keuchel-P	2	0	0	0	0	2	.000
B. Peacock-P	0	0	0	0	0	0	.000
C. Beltran-PH	1	0	0	0	0	0	.000
C. Devenski-P	0	0	0	0	0	0	.000
TEAM	30	1	3	1	0	12	

DODGERS

HITTERS	AB	R	H	RBI	BB	K	AVG
C. Taylor-CF	3	2	1	1	1	0	.333
J. Turner-3B	4	1	1	2	0	2	.250
C. Bellinger-1B	3	0	0	0	0	1	.000
Y. Puig-RF	3	0	0	0	0	0	.000
E. Hernandez-LF	3	0	1	0	0	1	.333
C. Seager-SS	3	0	2	0	0	0	.667
L. Forsythe-2B	2	0	0	0	1	0	.000
A. Barnes-C	3	0	1	0	0	0	.333
C. Kershaw-P	1	0	0	0	0	0	.000
B. Morrow-P	0	0	0	0	0	0	.000
C. Culberson-PH	1	0	0	0	0	1	.000
K. Jansen-P	0	0	0	0	0	0	.000
TEAM	26	3	6	3	2	5	

ASTROS

PITCHERS	IP	H	R	ER	BB	K	HR	ERA
D. Keuchel (L, 0-1)	6.2	6	3	3	1	3	2	4.05
B. Peacock	0.1	0	0	0	1	0	0	0.00
C. Devenski	1.0	0	0	0	0	2	0	0.00
TEAM	8.0	6	3	3	2	5	2	

DODGERS

PITCHERS	IP	H	R	ER	BB	K	HR	ERA
C. Kershaw (W, 1-0)	7.0	3	1	1	0	11	1	1.29
B. Morrow (H, 1)	1.0	0	0	0	0	0	0	0.00
K. Jansen (S, 1)	1.0	0	0	0	0	1	0	0.00
TEAM	9.0	3	1	1	0	12	1	

Carlos Correa and Jose Altuve
celebrate hitting back-to-back
home runs in the 10th inning.
AP Photo

OCTOBER 25, 2017   DODGERS STADIUM   LOS ANGELES, CALIFORNIA
HOUSTON ASTROS 7 • LOS ANGELES DODGERS 6

Astros outlast Dodgers in instant classic

George Springer celebrates as he rounds the bases following his game-winning two-run home run in the 11th inning. *AP Photo*

LOS ANGELES – Instant classic.

On one of the wildest nights in postseason history, George Springer hit a two-run homer in the 11th inning and the Houston Astros outlasted the Los Angeles Dodgers 7-6 to tie the series 1-1 and give the Astros their first-ever World Series win.

In a game where there were a World Series-record eight home runs, Marwin Gonzalez stunned the Dodger Stadium crowd with a solo shot off dominant Los Angeles closer Kenley Jansen on an 0-2 pitch in the ninth that made it 3-all.

In the bottom half of the inning rookie-of-the-year favorite Cody Bellinger brought

Marwin Gonzalez delivers a clutch solo home run in the top of the ninth inning to make it 3-3. *AP Photo*

the Dodger crowd back to its feet with a blast to the right-center field wall, just missing a walk-off home run.

Houston's all-star infielders Jose Altuve and Carlos Correa then hit back-to-back home runs against Dodger reliever (and former Astro) Josh Fields in the 10th to build a seemingly safe 5-3 Astros lead.

But there was more. Much, much more.

Yasiel Puig homered off Astros closer Ken Giles starting the bottom of the 10th and Enrique Hernandez knotted the score 5-5 with a two-out RBI single.

Cameron Maybin, who had entered the game in the 10th, singled leading off the 11th against losing pitcher Brandon McCarthy, a surprise addition to the Dodgers' World Series roster who was pitching for the first time since Oct. 1. Maybin stole second and Springer followed with his drive to right-center for a 7-5 lead.

Springer, an All-Star leadoff man, broke out of his slump with three hits and a walk after going 0 for 4 with four strikeouts in the Series opener.

The Dodgers made things interesting in the bottom half of the 11th as Charlie Culberson hit a two-out homer off Houston reliever Chris Devenski, who then struck out the dangerous Puig in a tense, nine-pitch at-bat.

"It was an emotional roller coaster," said Dodgers manager Dave Roberts, who removed starter Rich Hill after he threw only 60 pitches in four solid innings and struck out seven.

"We didn't expect these guys to lie down. It's a very good ballclub over there," Roberts said. "We'll be ready to go when we get to Houston for Game 3."

Houston starter Justin Verlander, wearing an undershirt after being taken out after six innings, entered the dugout in the ninth and screamed at his teammates that the game was not over.

"All of a sudden, two runs seemed like it was the Grand Canyon," he said. "I was just trying to remind these guys two runs is nothing. This was an instant classic and to be part of it is pretty special."

Alex Bregman's RBI single in the third gave Houston its first lead of the Series, a hit that might have turned into a three-run, inside-the-park homer had the ball not caromed off the bill of Dodger center fielder Chris Taylor's cap directly to left fielder Joc Pederson.

Los Angeles had just two hits through seven innings but led 3-1 behind Pederson's fifth-inning solo homer and Cory Seager's tiebreaking, two-run drive in the sixth against Verlander.

Jansen entered with a 3-1 lead trying for his first six-out save in a year after Bregman doubled leading off the eighth against Brandon Morrow, a ball that ticked off the glove of a diving Puig in the right-field corner.

Correa's RBI single off Jansen ended a record 28-inning postseason scoreless streak by the Dodgers' bullpen.

Gonzalez seemed an unlikely candidate for a tying homer. He had not driven in a run in his 45 plate appearances since Houston's playoff opener, and the blown save was just the second for Jansen this year. The Dodgers had been 98-0 in 2017 when leading after eight innings, including the postseason.

"I didn't make my pitch," Jansen said. "You can't beat yourself up about that."

Afterward, players were exhausted.

"When that last out is made, you finally breathe," Springer said. "That's an emotional high -- emotional high to low to high again. But that's why we play the game. And that's the craziest game that I've ever played in. And it's only Game 2."

BOX SCORE

	1	2	3	4	5	6	7	8	9	10	11	R	H	E
HOU	0	0	1	0	0	0	0	1	1	2	2	7	14	1
LAD	0	0	0	0	1	2	0	0	0	2	1	6	5	0

ASTROS

HITTERS	AB	R	H	RBI	BB	K	AVG
G. Springer-CF-RF	5	1	3	2	1	0	.333
A. Bregman-3B	6	1	2	1	0	0	.300
J. Altuve-2B	6	1	1	1	0	2	.200
C. Correa-SS	6	1	3	2	0	1	.333
Y. Gurriel-1B	4	0	1	0	1	0	.143
B. McCann-C	5	0	0	0	0	2	.000
M. Gonzalez-LF	3	1	1	1	2	2	.167
J. Reddick-RF	4	1	1	0	1	0	.286
C. Devenski-P	0	0	0	0	0	0	.000
J. Verlander-P	1	0	0	0	0	1	.000
E. Gattis-PH	1	0	1	0	0	0	1.000
W. Harris-P	0	0	0	0	0	0	.000
J. Musgrove-P	0	0	0	0	0	0	.000
C. Beltran-PH	1	0	0	0	0	0	.000
K. Giles-P	0	0	0	0	0	0	.000
C. Maybin-CF	1	1	1	0	0	0	1.000
TEAM	43	7	14	7	5	8	

DODGERS

HITTERS	AB	R	H	RBI	BB	K	AVG
C. Taylor-CF	3	1	0	0	2	1	.167
B. McCarthy-P	0	0	0	0	0	0	.000
C. Seager-SS	5	1	1	2	0	2	.375
J. Turner-3B	5	0	0	0	0	0	.111
C. Bellinger-1B	4	0	0	0	0	2	.000
T. Cingrani-P	0	0	0	0	0	0	.000
C. Culberson-LF	1	1	1	1	0	0	.500
Y. Puig-RF	5	1	1	1	0	1	.125
J. Pederson-LF	3	1	1	1	0	2	.333
K. Jansen-P	0	0	0	0	0	0	.000
J. Fields-P	0	0	0	0	0	0	.000
Y. Grandal-C	1	0	0	0	0	1	.000
A. Barnes-C-2B	4	0	0	0	0	2	.143
C. Utley-2B	3	0	0	0	0	0	.000
L. Forsythe-2B-1B	0	1	0	0	1	0	.000
R. Hill-P	1	0	0	0	0	0	.000
K. Maeda-P	0	0	0	0	0	0	.000
T. Watson-P	0	0	0	0	0	0	.000
A. Ethier-PH	1	0	0	0	0	0	.000
R. Stripling-P	0	0	0	0	0	0	.000
B. Morrow-P	0	0	0	0	0	0	.000
E. Hernandez-LF-CF	2	0	1	1	0	0	.400
TEAM	26	3	6	3	2	5	

ASTROS

	IP	H	R	ER	BB	K	HR	ERA
J. Verlander	6.0	2	3	3	2	5	2	4.50
W. Harris	1.0	0	0	0	0	2	0	0.00
J. Musgrove	1.0	0	0	0	0	0	0	0.00
K. Giles	1.2	2	2	2	1	3	1	10.80
C. Devenski (W, 1-0)	1.1	1	1	1	0	1	1	3.86
TEAM	11.0	5	6	6	3	11	4Å	

DODGERS

PITCHERS	IP	H	R	ER	BB	K	HR	ERA
R. Hill	4.0	3	1	1	3	7	0	2.25
K. Maeda	1.1	1	0	0	0	0	0	0.00
T. Watson	0.2	0	0	0	0	0	0	0.00
R. Stripling	0.0	0	0	0	1	0	0	0.00
B. Morrow (H, 2)	1.0	2	1	1	0	0	0	4.50
K. Jansen (B, 1)	2.0	3	1	1	0	1	1	3.00
J. Fields	0.0	3	2	2	0	0	2	INF
T. Cingrani	1.0	0	0	0	1	0	0	0.00
B. McCarthy (L, 0-1)	1.0	2	2	2	0	0	1	18.00
TEAM	11.0	14	7	7	5	8	4	

Yuli Gurriel hits a second inning home run off Dodgers starting pitcher Yu Darvish.
AP Photo

OCTOBER 27, 2017   MINUTE MAID PARK   HOUSTON, TEXAS
HOUSTON ASTROS 5 • LOS ANGELES DODGERS 3

Home Sweet Home

Houston right fielder Josh Reddick slides safely past Dodgers catcher Austin Barnes after a wild throw by reliever Tony Watson during fifth inning action. *AP Photo*

HOUSTON -- A perfect fit in their own place, the Houston Astros are halfway home.

Yuli Gurriel and the Astros broke out the bats early this time to keep up their unbeaten October run at spirited Minute Maid Park, beating the Los Angeles Dodgers 5-3 Friday night for a 2-1 lead in the World Series.

"We're very comfortable here," Astros manager A.J. Hinch said.

You can say that again.

Coming off a dramatic rally to win Game 2 at Dodger Stadium, the Astros improved to 7-0 at home this postseason. Jose Altuve & Co. have dominated, too, outscoring the Red Sox, Yankees and Dodgers 36-10 in that span.

Gurriel homered into the Crawford Boxes in left to begin a four-run burst in the second. Josh Reddick followed with a double and Evan Gattis, the designated hitter with the game in an American League park, drew a walk.

Marwin Gonzalez launched a drive off the wall in left-center and wound up with an RBI single when Gattis held at second, seeing if the ball would be caught. Brian McCann singled home another run with

one of his three hits, and Alex Bregman's sacrifice fly made it 4-0.

When Altuve doubled, Dodges starter Yu Darvish was done after 1 2/3 innings. He threw 49 pitches and the Astros swung and missed only once.

Darvish had done well at Minute Maid, going 4-1. That included a 2013 start when he was one out from a perfect game for the Rangers before Gonzalez singled.

"The fastball command wasn't there, and the slider was backing up. So he just really didn't have the feel and couldn't get any type of rhythm going," Dodgers manager Dave Roberts said.

Astros starting pitcher Lance McCullers Jr. left in the sixth as Los Angeles scored twice to cut into a 5-1 deficit.

Brad Peacock followed, and shouldered the load for a shaky bullpen. The right-hander was nearly perfect, walking one and striking out four in 3 2/3 innings.

With every pitch by Peacock in the ninth, the decibel level increased.

"It was awesome," said Peacock, who made 21 starts and 13 relief appearances during the regular season. "I've never experienced anything like that in my life."

"Obviously, this crowd is into it. Very educated, very enthusiastic," Roberts said. "They've got some confidence over there, that team."

On a night when a lot went right for Houston, also credit third base coach Gary Pettis, who's been having quite a postseason. He boldly sent Reddick careening home on a wild throw by reliever Tony Watson for a two-out run in the fifth.

This game wasn't nearly as dramatic as the previous one, not that the home crowd minded.

Fans were revved up from the start when injured Houston Texas defensive end J.J. Watt -- who has raised more than $37 million for relief efforts after Hurricane Harvey -- hobbled out to the mound on

crutches to throw the first pitch.

Deep in the heart of football country, a sellout crowd stood much of the evening. And with every Houston batter getting a hit or walk, fans enjoyed the Friday Night Sights.

"The energy in the building is second to none," Hinch said. "It's loud. They're loud from the very beginning."

Astros reliever Brad Peacock shakes hands with catcher Brian McCann after picking up his first big league save in Game 3. *AP Photo*

BOX SCORE

	1	2	3	4	5	6	7	8	9	R	H	E
LAD	0	0	1	0	0	2	0	0	0	3	4	2
HOU	0	4	0	0	1	0	0	0	-	5	12	0

DODGERS

HITTERS	AB	R	H	RBI	BB	K	AVG
C. Taylor-CF	3	0	0	0	1	0	.111
C. Seager-SS	3	1	0	0	1	1	.273
J. Turner-3B	4	1	1	0	0	0	.154
C. Bellinger-1B	4	0	0	0	0	4	.000
Y. Puig-RF	4	0	1	1	0	1	.167
L. Forsythe-2B	2	0	1	0	0	0	.250
C. Utley-PH-2B	2	0	0	0	0	0	.000
A. Barnes-C	2	0	0	0	0	0	.111
Y. Grandal-PH-C	2	0	0	0	0	0	.000
J. Pederson-DH	2	1	1	0	1	1	.400
E. Hernandez-LF	1	0	0	0	1	0	.333
A. Ethier-PH-LF	0	0	0	0	1	0	.333
TEAM	29	3	4	1	5	7	

ASTROS

HITTERS	AB	R	H	RBI	BB	K	AVG
G. Springer-CF	5	0	1	0	0	1	.286
A. Bregman-3B	3	0	0	1	1	1	.231
J. Altuve-2B	5	0	1	0	0	2	.200
C. Correa-SS	5	0	1	0	0	1	.286
Y. Gurriel-1B	5	1	2	1	0	0	.250
J. Reddick-RF	4	2	2	0	0	0	.364
E. Gattis-DH	1	1	1	1	3	0	1.000
M. Gonzalez-LF	4	1	1	1	0	1	.200
B. McCann-C	4	0	3	1	0	0	.250
TEAM	36	5	12	4	4	6	

DODGERS

PITCHERS	IP	H	R	ER	BB	K	HR	ERA
Y. Darvish (L, 0-1)	1.2	6	4	4	1	0	1	21.60
K. Maeda	2.2	1	0	0	1	2	0	0.00
T. Watson	1.0	2	1	0	0	1	0	0.00
B. Morrow	0.2	1	0	0	1	2	0	3.38
T. Cingrani	0.2	1	0	0	1	0	0	0.00
R. Stripling	1.1	1	0	0	0	1	0	0.00
TEAM	8.0	12	5	4	4	6	1	

ASTROS

PITCHERS	IP	H	R	ER	BB	K	HR	ERA
L. McCullers Jr. (W, 1-0)	5.1	4	3	3	4	3	5.06	
B. Peacock (S, 1)	3.2	0	0	0	1	4	0	0.00
TEAM	9.0	4	3	3	5	7	0	

Joc Pederson hits a three-run
home run off Houston relief
pitcher Joe Musgrove in the
ninth inning to break open
Game 4. *AP Photo*

OCTOBER 28, 2017   MINUTE MAID PARK   HOUSTON, TEXAS
HOUSTON ASTROS 2 • LOS ANGELES DODGERS 6

Dodgers rally late to even World Series

George Springer celebrates after giving the Astros a 1-0 lead with his sixth inning home run. *AP Photo*

HOUSTON – When the Los Angeles Dodgers needed him most Cody Bellinger delivered.

Hitless in 13 at-bats, Bellinger doubled and scored the tying run in the seventh inning on a two-out single by Logan Forsythe. He then doubled home the go-ahead run off struggling Houston Astros closer Ken Giles in a five-run ninth that lifted the Dodgers to a 6-2 win and tied the Series at two games apiece.

"Sometimes in the postseason to try to do too much, and that's what I was doing," Bellinger said.

The Dodgers Austin Barnes is caught in a rundown and tagged out by Astros catcher Brian McCann during sixth inning action. *AP Photo*

George Springer put the Astros ahead with a two-out homer in the sixth, the first hit off Los Angeles starter Alex Wood. The crowd at Minute Maid Park, where Houston had been 7-0 this postseason, was revved up in anticipation of the Astros having a chance to win the first title in their 56-season history.

Instead, the Series will go back to Los Angeles no matter what. Clayton Kershaw starts Game 5 for the Dodgers and Dallas Keuchel for the Astros in a rematch of the opener, when Kershaw pitched Los Angeles to a 3-1 win.

Giles entered to start the ninth and got into immediate trouble, allowing a leadoff single to Corey Seager and a walk to Justin Turner. Bellinger took a low slider, then lined a fastball at the letters to left-center.

"Every day you see him grow a little bit more," Wood said of the Dodger rookie. "I think everybody kind of had the same message with him: `We believe in you. You're our guy. You're special. Remember that."

Joe Musgrove relieved Giles and allowed Austin Barnes' sacrifice fly and Joc Pederson's three-run homer, his second home run of the Series.

Wood, Brandon Morrow, winner Tony Watson and Kenley Jansen combined on a two-hitter -- the first-ever in the Series in which both hits were home runs. Jansen allowed Alex Bregman's two-out long ball in the ninth, the 15th home run of the Series, most ever through four games, before retiring Jose Altuve on a flyout.

Giles, the loser, was charged with three runs.

"They were all crappy pitches, not where I wanted them," he said. "I need to do better. I need to pick up this team. I need to carry my weight."

He has an 11.75 postseason ERA, allowing runs in six of seven appearances.

"When you're a back-end reliever," Astros manager A.J. Hinch said, "unless you're extraordinarily dominant, you're only talked about when you suffer, when you struggle. So for him, he can handle it mentally. He can handle it physically."

Springer put the Astros ahead when he drove a curveball, Wood's 84th and final pitch, over the left-field scoreboard and into the Crawford Boxes. Wood dropped to a knee on the mound and watched the ball land in the seats and rebound onto the field.

Houston was nine outs from winning for the 18th time in 20 home games since returning to Minute Maid Park after Hurricane Harvey, and from becoming the first major league team to start a postseason 8-0 at home.

In the team's 109th World Series game, Wood became the first Dodgers pitcher to hold an opponent hitless through five innings.

Morton was nearly as stingy, allowing three hits in 6 1/3 innings. This was the first Series game in which both starters allowed four baserunners or fewer.

BOX SCORE

	1	2	3	4	5	6	7	8	9	R	H	E
LAD	0	0	0	0	0	0	1	0	5	6	7	0
HOU	0	0	0	0	0	1	0	0	1	2	2	0

DODGERS

HITTERS	AB	R	H	RBI	BB	K	AVG
C. Taylor-CF	4	0	1	0	0	1	.154
C. Seager-SS	4	1	1	0	0	1	.267
J. Turner-3B	3	0	0	0	1	1	.125
C. Culberson-PR-2B	0	1	0	0	0	0	.500
C. Bellinger-1B	4	2	2	1	0	1	.133
Y. Puig-RF	4	0	0	0	0	1	.125
L. Forsythe-2B-3B	3	1	1	1	1	1	.286
A. Barnes-C	2	0	0	1	0	0	.091
J. Pederson-DH	4	1	1	3	0	2	.333
E. Hernandez-LF	4	0	1	0	0	1	.300
TEAM	32	6	7	6	2	9	

ASTROS

HITTERS	AB	R	H	RBI	BB	K	AVG
G. Springer-CF	4	1	1	1	0	1	.278
A. Bregman-3B	4	1	1	1	0	0	.235
J. Altuve-2B	4	0	0	0	0	0	.158
C. Correa-SS	2	0	0	0	1	0	.250
Y. Gurriel-1B	3	0	0	0	0	1	.200
J. Reddick-RF	3	0	0	0	0	0	.286
E. Gattis-DH	3	0	0	0	0	0	.400
M. Gonzalez-LF	2	0	0	0	1	0	.167
B. McCann-C	3	0	0	0	0	2	.200
TEAM	28	2	2	2	2	4	

DODGERS

PITCHERS	IP	H	R	ER	BB	K	HR	ERA
A. Wood	5.2	1	1	1	2	3	1	1.59
B. Morrow	1.1	0	0	0	0	0	0	2.25
T. Watson (W, 1-0)	1.0	0	0	0	0	0	0	0.00
K. Jansen	1.0	1	1	1	0	1	1	4.50
TEAM	9.0	2	2	2	2	4	2	

ASTROS

PITCHERS	IP	H	R	ER	BB	K	HR	ERA
C. Morton	6.1	3	1	1	0	7	0	1.42
W. Harris (B, 1)	0.2	1	0	0	0	0	0	0.00
C. Devenski	1.0	0	0	0	0	1	0	2.70
K. Giles (L, 0-1)	0.0	2	3	3	1	0	0	27.00
J. Musgrove	1.0	1	2	2	1	1	1	9.00
TEAM	9.0	7	6	6	2	9	1	

"The innings were rolling pretty quickly there the first four, five, six innings," Wood said. "It kept both of us locked in."

Alex Bregman delivers the game-winning hit off Dodgers reliever Kenley Jansen in the bottom of the 10th inning. *AP Photo*

OCTOBER 29, 2017 MINUTE MAID PARK HOUSTON, TEXAS
HOUSTON ASTROS 13 • LOS ANGELES DODGERS 12

Astros win wild one 13-12

Astros pinch runner Derek Fisher races home with the game-winning run as teammate Alex Correa looks on. *AP Photo*

HOUSTON – Where to begin?

In one of the epic games in an unforgettable Fall Classic the never-say-die Houston Astros did it again.

Alex Bregman hit a walk-off single into left field off Los Angeles Dodgers closer Kenley Jansen in the 10th inning to score pinch-runner Derek Fisher from second base and put an end to the second-longest World Series game in history, sending the Astros to a dramatic 13-12 victory and a 3-2 lead in the series.

Carlos Correa, Jose Altuve and the Astros kept hammering away in a wild slugfest, rallying after falling behind 4-0 against Dodgers ace Clayton Kershaw.

Exhilaration and exhaustion, spread over 5 hours, 17 minutes.

"Yeah, five-hour game, but it doesn't matter. I can play a 10-hour game if we are going to win," Altuve said.

Altuve, Correa, Yuli Gurriel, George Springer and Brian McCann homered for Houston, the highest-scoring team in the majors this season.

Cody Bellinger and Yasiel Puig went deep

Yuli Gurriel watches his three-run home run off Dodgers starting pitcher Clayton Kershaw leave the park. The fourth inning blast tied the score 4-4. *AP Photo*

for the Dodgers, who scored three times in the ninth to make it 12-all.

"It's hard to put into words all the twists and turns in that game," Astros manager A.J. Hinch said.

"These are just two really good teams, just throwing haymakers at each other trying to outlast each other," he said.

Silent when ace Dallas Keuchel got crushed, the orange-clad fans erupted over and over as the Astros sent balls careening all around -- and out of -- the park.

On this night no lead was safe.

Puig lined a two-run shot in the ninth, the record 22nd homer in a single Series, and Chris Taylor's two-out single off Chris Devenski tied it.

"I think this whole series has been an emotional roller coaster," Dodgers manager Dave Roberts said. "It's the two best teams playing for a championship. And these are two teams that play 27 outs."

Houston posted its second extra-inning victory of the Series, adding to its 7-6, 11-inning comeback win in a dramatic Game 2.

The Astros climbed out of a four-run hole against Kershaw and then erased two more deficits later in the game, tying it each time on a homer.

Correa leaped and twirled after launching a two-run drive that made it 11-8 in the seventh. Much later, he hurdled the dugout railing the moment Bregman lined his winning single.

Rookie sensation Cody Bellinger hit a three-run drive in the fifth that made it 7-4 and seemed to swing things back in the Dodgers' favor. By the end of the mayhem on the mound, it was a mere afterthought.

Each team had 14 hits, eight for extra bases, and both used seven pitchers.

"Just exactly what you expect (when you) come to the park with Keuchel and Kershaw pitching," Hinch said with a smile.

Keuchel never got into a rhythm during the shortest home start of his All-Star career. His breaking pitches spun without much movement, and he was pulled in the fourth.

The Dodgers hadn't lost a game this year when they led by four runs. But Kershaw's bedeviling postseason past came back to haunt him at the worst time.

Kershaw was pulled after a pair of two-out walks in the bottom of the fifth. And with the

crowd sensing something big, the 5-foot-6 Altuve connected off Kenta Maeda for a home run that made it 7-all.

"At that point, I talked to him before getting the at-bat: `This is your moment,"
Correa said. "And he didn't let me down."

BOX SCORE

	1	2	3	4	5	6	7	8	9	10	R	H	E
LAD	3	0	0	1	3	0	1	1	3	0	12	14	1
HOU	0	0	0	4	3	0	4	1	0	1	13	14	1

DODGERS

HITTERS	AB	R	H	RBI	BB	K	AVG
C. Taylor-CF	5	1	2	1	0	1	.222
C. Seager-SS	5	1	1	1	1	2	.250
J. Turner-DH	4	2	1	0	2	0	.150
E. Hernandez-LF-2b	3	2	0	0	1	1	.231
A. Ethier-PH-LF	2	0	1	0	0	0	.333
C. Bellinger-1B	5	2	2	4	1	2	.200
L. Forsythe-3B	6	1	2	2	0	2	.308
Y. Puig-RF	5	1	1	2	0	2	.143
A. Barnes-C	5	1	2	1	0	2	.188
C. Culberson-2B	2	0	1	0	0	0	.500
J. Pederson-PH-LF-CF	2	1	1	0	1	0	.364
TEAM	**44**	**12**	**14**	**11**	**6**	**12**	

ASTROS

HITTERS	AB	R	H	RBI	BB	K	AVG
G. Springer-CF-RF	3	3	2	1	3	0	.333
A. Bregman-3B	5	2	2	1	1	0	.273
J. Altuve-2B	5	3	3	4	0	1	.250
C. Correa-SS	5	2	3	3	0	0	.333
Y. Gurriel-1B	5	1	2	3	0	1	.250
C. Maybin-PR-CF	0	0	0	0	0	0	1.000
J. Reddick-RF-LF	5	0	0	0	0	2	.211
E. Gattis-DH	4	0	1	0	1	0	.333
M. Gonzalez-LF-1B	5	0	0	0	0	1	.118
B. McCann-C	4	1	1	1	0	1	.211
D. Fisher-PR	0	1	0	0	0	0	.000
TEAM	**41**	**13**	**14**	**13**	**5**	**6**	

DODGERS

C. Kershaw	4.2	4	6	6	3	2	1	5.40
K. Maeda	0.2	2	1	1	1	1	1	1.93
T. Watson	0.2	0	0	0	0	0	0	0.00
B. Morrow (B, 1)	0.0	4	4	4	0	0	2	11.25
T. Cingrani	1.1	1	1	1	0	2	1	3.00
R. Stripling	0.2	1	0	0	0	0	0	0.00
K. Jansen (L, 0-1)	1.2	2	1	1	1	1	0	4.76
TEAM	**9.2**	**14**	**13**	**13**	**5**	**6**	**5**	

ASTROS

D. Keuchel	3.2	5	4	3	2	4	0	5.23
L. Gregerson	0.1	0	0	0	0	1	0	0.00
C. McHugh	2.0	1	3	3	3	4	1	13.50
B. Peacock	1.1	3	2	2	0	2	0	3.38
W. Harris (H, 1)	0.1	1	0	0	0	0	0	0.00
C. Devenski (B, 1)	1.1	3	3	3	1	1	1	7.71
J. Musgrove (W, 1-0)	1.0	1	0	0	0	0	0	6.00
TEAM	**10.0**	**14**	**12**	**11**	**6**	**12**	**2**	

Catcher Brian McCann is congratulated with a bag full of sunflower seeds on his head after hitting a big eighth inning home run. *AP Photo*

George Springer drives a third inning pitch over the wall to give the Astros a 1-0 lead. *AP Photo*

OCTOBER 31, 2017   DODGERS STADIUM   LOS ANGELES, CALIFORNIA
HOUSTON ASTROS 1 • LOS ANGELES DODGERS 3

Dodgers force Game 7

The Dodgers Chris Taylor delivers a clutch RBI double down the right field line off starting pitcher Justin Verlander that tied the score 1-1 in the sixth inning. *AP Photo*

LOS ANGELES – On a night when treats were handed out to children across the country baseball fans might have received the best treat of them all – a Game 7.

The Los Angeles Dodgers kept their World Series hopes alive with a crucial 3-1 win over the Houston Astros in Game 6, setting the stage for a deciding Game 7 before their home crowd.

"I think it seems fitting," Dodgers manager Dave Roberts said about this series needing all seven games. "You've got the two best teams in baseball going head to head. Like we've talked

Astros manager A.J. Hinch talks to his team as the Dodgers threaten in the sixth inning. *AP Photo*

about from the beginning, these two teams mirror one another. They both compete and fight. But we worked all year long to have home-field advantage, and here we are."

Los Angeles is hoping for its first World Series win since 1988, while Houston is seeking its first-ever.

Game 6 started with a little less firepower than the epic Game 5 that saw a combined 25 runs, including seven home runs, in 10 innings.

George Springer's third-inning home run against starter Rich Hill had given a 1-0 lead to starter Justin Verlander and the Astros, but it served only to set up the 10th blown lead of the Series. Verlander ended up going six innings, allowing two runs on three hits while striking out nine. He fell to 9-1 with the Astros.

The Dodgers' scoring started in the sixth inning with an RBI single by

Chris Taylor and a sacrifice fly by Corey Seager.

A solo home run by Joc Pederson off Joe Musgrove put the Dodgers up 3-1 in the seventh. Pederson connected off the right-hander for the second time in three games and made it a record 24 long balls that have been hit in this Series. Pederson pranced all the way to the plate, pointing at the Dodgers' dugout and rubbing his thumbs and index fingers together to indicate what a money shot it was.

"You kind of black out in a situation like that. So I'm going to have to re-watch it to see what I did," Pederson said.

Manager Dave Roberts decided to pull Hill with the bases loaded and two outs in the fifth. Hill had given up Brian McCann's leadoff single and Marwin Gonzalez's ensuing double, but then struck out Josh Reddick and Justin Verlander to get to the brink of escaping the jam.

Instead, Roberts ordered an intentional walk for George Springer and then turned the game over to his bullpen.

Reliever Brandon Morrow retired Alex Bregman on a grounder to strand the bases loaded in the fifth. Winner Tony Watson got Marwin Gonzalez to line out to leaping second baseman Chase Utley with two on and two outs in the sixth, and Kenta Maeda escaped two-on trouble in the seventh when third baseman Justin Turner gloved Jose Altuve's grounder and made a short-hop throw that first baseman Cody Bellinger scooped just in time.

"That pick by Bellinger was big," Houston manager A.J. Hinch said. "Fifth, sixth, seventh inning we had pressure on them, but they made pitches and made plays."

BOX SCORE

	1	2	3	4	5	6	7	8	9	R	H	E
HOU	0	0	1	0	0	0	0	0	0	1	6	0
LAD	0	0	0	0	0	2	1	0	-	3	5	0

ASTROS

HITTERS	AB	R	H	RBI	BB	K	AVG
G. Springer-CF	3	1	2	1	1	1	.375
A. Bregman-3B	4	0	1	0	0	0	.269
J. Altuve-2B	4	0	0	0	0	1	.214
C. Correa-SS	4	0	0	0	0	1	.280
Y. Gurriel-1B	4	0	1	0	0	0	.250
B. McCann-C	3	0	1	0	0	1	.227
M. Gonzalez-LF	4	0	1	0	0	0	.143
J. Reddick-RF	3	0	0	0	1	2	.182
J. Verlander-P	2	0	0	0	0	2	.000
E. Gattis-PH	1	0	0	0	0	0	.300
D. Fisher-PR	0	0	0	0	0	0	.000
J. Musgrove-P	0	0	0	0	0	0	.000
L. Gregerson-P	0	0	0	0	0	0	.000
F. Liriano-P	0	0	0	0	0	0	.000
C. Beltran-PH	1	0	0	0	0	1	.000
TEAM	33	1	6	1	2	9	

DODGERS

HITTERS	AB	R	H	RBI	BB	K	AVG
C. Taylor-CF	4	0	1	1	0	1	.227
C. Seager-SS	3	0	0	1	0	2	.217
J. Turner-3B	3	0	0	0	1	1	.130
C. Bellinger-1B	4	0	0	0	0	4	.167
Y. Puig-RF	3	0	1	0	0	0	.167
J. Pederson-LF	3	1	1	1	0	1	.357
L. Forsythe-2B	2	0	0	0	0	1	.267
T. Watson-P	0	0	0	0	0	0	.000
K. Maeda-P	0	0	0	0	0	0	.000
A. Ethier-PH	1	0	0	0	0	0	.250
K. Jansen-P	0	0	0	0	0	0	.000
A. Barnes-C	3	1	1	0	0	1	.211
R. Hill-P	1	0	0	0	0	1	.000
B. Morrow-P	0	0	0	0	0	0	.000
C. Utley-2B	0	1	0	0	0	0	.000
C. Culberson-2B	1	0	1	0	0	0	.600
TEAM	28	3	5	3	1	12	

ASTROS

PITCHERS	IP	H	R	ER	BB	K	HR	ERA
J. Verlander (L, 0-1)	6.0	3	2	2	0	9	0	3.75
J. Musgrove	1.0	1	1	1	0	1	1	6.75
L. Gregerson	0.2	1	0	0	1	1	0	0.00
F. Liriano	0.1	0	0	0	0	1	0	0.00
TEAM	8.0	5	3	3	1	12	1	

DODGERS

PITCHERS	IP	H	R	ER	BB	K	HR	ERA
R. Hill	4.2	4	1	1	1	5	1	2.08
B. Morrow	1.0	1	0	0	0	1	0	9.00
T. Watson (W, 2-0)	0.1	0	0	0	1	0	0	0.00
K. Maeda (H, 1)	1.0	1	0	0	0	0	0	1.59
K. Jansen (S, 2)	2.0	0	0	0	0	3	0	3.52
TEAM	9.0	6	1	1	2	9	1	

Catcher Brian McCann jumps into the arms of pitcher Charlie Morton after getting the final out of Game 7. *AP Photo*

NOVEMBER 1, 2017   DODGERS STADIUM   LOS ANGELES, CALIFORNIA
HOUSTON ASTROS 5 • LOS ANGELES DODGERS 1

World Champions!

Winning pitcher Charlie Morton is mobbed by his teammates after winning Game 7. *AP Photo*

LOS ANGELES – Believe it Houston. George Springer and the Houston Astros rocketed to the top of the baseball galaxy winning the first World Series championship in franchise history by romping past the Los Angeles Dodgers 5-1 in Game 7.

Playing for a city still recovering from Hurricane Harvey, and wearing an H Strong logo on their jerseys, the Astros brought home the prize that had eluded them since they started out in 1962 as the Colt .45s.

"I always believed that we could make it," All-Star second baseman Jose Altuve said. "We did this for them."

For a Series that was shaping up

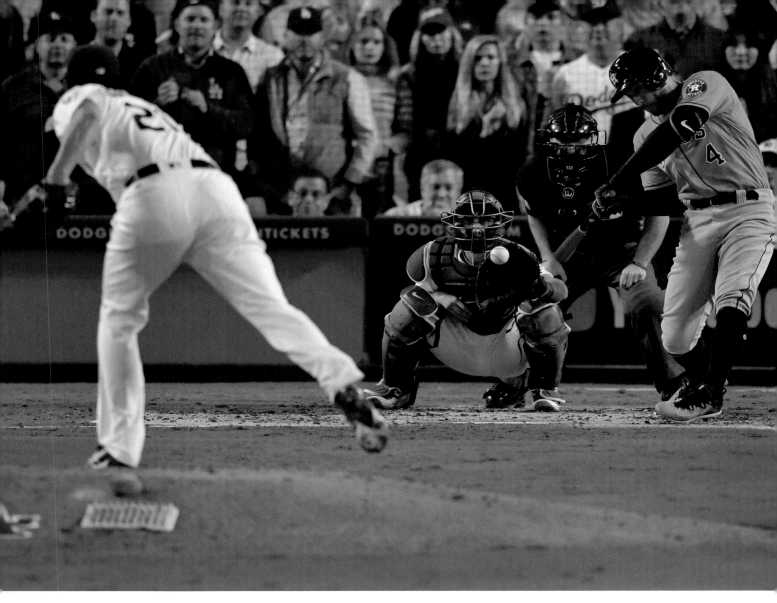

World Series MVP George Springer blasts a two-run home run off Dodgers starting pitcher Yu Darvish. It was Springer's fifth home run of the Series. *AP Photo*

as an October classic, Game 7 quickly became a November clunker as Houston scored five runs in the first two innings off an ineffective Yu Darvish. Hardly the excitement fans felt during the Cubs' 10-inning thriller in Cleveland last fall.

Well, except for everyone wearing bright orange.

"We're coming home a champion, Houston," Springer said after accepting the World Series MVP trophy named this year after Willie Mays for the first time.

Altuve, one of four carry-overs from a club that lost an embarrassing 111 times in 2013 after switching from the NL to the

AL, and this collection of young stars silenced Dodger Stadium from the get-go.

After Springer lined a leadoff double, Alex Bregman hit a bouncer that first baseman Cody Bellinger threw past Darvish for an error, allowing a run to score. Bregman aggressively stole third and scored on Altuve's grounder, and it was 2-0 after eight pitches.

A double by Marwin Gonzalez helped set up perhaps starting pitcher Lance McCullers' biggest contribution, a slow grounder for his first pro RBI. Springer followed with a no-doubt, two-run drive into the left-center field bleachers to make it 5-0.

It was Springer's fifth homer -- tying the Series mark set by Reggie Jackson and matched by Chase Utley -- and he connected for a record fourth game in a row.

Upon receiving his MVP award, Springer spoke about how the Series victory was especially meaningful both for the franchise and the city.

"This is a dream come true and an honor," Springer said. "But it's about the Houston Astros tonight, our city, our fans. That Houston Strong patch on our chests really does mean something."

Houston manager A.J. Hinch pulled starter McCullers Jr. soon after the curveballer crazily plunked his fourth batter of the game, and began a bullpen parade of four relievers that kept the lead as the Astros overcame a shaky postseason bullpen.

Normally a starter, Charlie Morton finished up with four stellar innings of relief for the win.

"We held down a really tough lineup," Morton said. "For my teammates, for the city of Houston, it's just unbelievable."

Forever known for their space-age Astrodome, outlandish rainbow jerseys and a handful of heartbreaking playoff losses, these Astros will be remembered as champions, finally, in their 56th season.

Built on the skills of homegrown All-Stars Carlos Correa, Dallas Keuchel and more, and boosted by the slick trade for Justin Verlander, general manager Jeff Luhnow completed the ascent that some predicted.

Houston won 101 times this year to take the AL West, then won Games 6 and 7 at home in the AL Championship Series. The Astros joined the 1985 Royals as the only clubs to win a pair of Game 7s in the same year.

As pockets of Houston fans got louder and louder in the later innings, the crowd at Dodger Stadium was left to repeat the sad, but hopeful cry that used to echo in Brooklyn: Wait till next year.

BOX SCORE

	1	2	3	4	5	6	7	8	9	R	H	E
HOU	2	3	1	0	0	0	0	0	0	5	5	0
LAD	0	0	0	0	0	1	0	0	0	1	6	1

ASTROS

HITTERS	AB	R	H	RBI	BB	K	AVG
G. Springer-CF-RF	5	2	2	2	0	1	.379
A. Bregman-3B	4	1	0	0	0	3	.233
J. Altuve-2B	3	0	0	1	1	0	.194
C. Correa-SS	4	0	1	0	0	0	.276
Y. Gurriel-1B	4	0	0	0	0	1	.214
B. McCann-C	3	1	0	0	1	2	.200
M. Gonzalez-LF	3	1	2	0	1	0	.208
J. Reddick-F	2	0	0	0	0	0	.167
E. Gattis-PH	0	0	0	0	1	0	.300
C. Morton-P	1	0	0	0	0	1	.000
L. McCullers Jr.-P	1	0	0	1	0	0	.000
B. Peacock-P	1	0	0	0	0	0	.000
F. Liriano-P	0	0	0	0	0	0	.000
C. Devenski-P	0	0	0	0	0	0	.000
C. Maybin-PH-CF	2	0	0	0	0	1	.333
TEAM	33	5	5	4	4	9	

DODGERS

HITTERS	AB	R	H	RBI	BB	K	AVG
C. Taylor-CF	5	0	1	0	0	1	.22
C. Seager-SS	4	0	1	0	1	1	.222
J. Turner-3B	2	0	1	0	0	0	.160
C. Bellinger-1B	4	0	0	0	0	3	.143
Y. Puig-RF	3	0	0	0	0	0	.148
J. Pederson-LF	4	1	1	0	0	2	.333
L. Forsythe-2B	3	0	1	0	1	0	.278
A. Barnes-C	4	0	0	0	0	0	.174
Y. Darvish-P	0	0	0	0	0	0	.000
B. Morrow-P	0	0	0	0	0	0	.000
E. Hernandez-PH	0	0	0	0	0	0	.231
C. Kershaw-P	1	0	0	0	0	1	.000
A. Ethier-PH	1	0	1	1	0	0	.400
K. Jansen-P	0	0	0	0	0	0	.000
A. Wood-P	0	0	0	0	0	0	.000
C. Utley-PH	1	0	0	0	0	1	.000
TEAM	32	1	6	1	2	9	

ASTROS

PITCHERS	IP	H	R	ER	BB	K	HR	ERA
L. McCullers Jr.	2.1	3	0	0	0	3	0	3.52
B. Peacock	2.0	1	0	0	1	2	0	2.45
F. Liriano	0.1	0	0	0	0	0	0	0.00
C. Devenski	0.1	0	0	0	0	0	0	7.20
C. Morton (W, 1-0)	4.0	2	1	1	1	4	0	1.74
TEAM	9.0	6	1	1	2	9	0	

DODGERS

	IP	H	R	ER	BB	K	HR	ERA
Y. Darvish (L, 0-2)	1.2	3	5	4	1	0	1	21.60
B. Morrow	0.1	0	0	0	0	1	0	8.44
C. Kershaw	4.0	2	0	0	2	4	0	4.02
K. Jansen	1.0	0	0	0	1	1	0	3.12
A. Wood	2.0	0	0	0	0	3	0	1.17
TEAM	9.0	5	5	4	4	9	1